THE GOOD LIFE

THE GOOD LIFE

You Can Walk in God's Perfect Will

JEFFREY M. MAGADA

 Please note that Destiny Image's publishing style capitalizes certain pronouns in Scripture that refer to the Father, Son, and Holy Spirit, and may differ from some publishers' styles. Take note that the name satan and related names are not capitalized. We choose not to acknowledge him, even to the point of violating grammatical rules.

DESTINY IMAGE® PUBLISHERS, INC.
P.O. Box 310, Shippensburg, PA 17257-0310

"Speaking to the Purposes of God for This Generation and for the Generations to Come."

This book and all other Destiny Image, Revival Press, MercyPlace, Fresh Bread, Destiny Image Fiction, and Treasure House books are available at Christian bookstores and distributors worldwide.

For a U.S. bookstore nearest you, call 1-800-722-6774.
For more information on foreign distributors, call 717-532-3040.
Reach us on the Internet: www.destinyimage.com.

Trade Paper ISBN 13: 978-0-7684-3097-4
Hardcover ISBN 13: 978-0-7684-3578-8
Larg Print ISBN 13: 978-0-7684-3579-5
Ebook ISBN 13: 978-0-7684-9561-4

For Worldwide Distribution, Printed in the U.S.A.

1 2 3 4 5 6 7 8 9 10 11 / 15 14 13 12 11

Dedication

To my mom, Sylvia M. Magada. It was her prayers that brought me into God's perfect will for my life.

To my grandfather, Joseph Lalama. He supported me when no one else would.

To those who have helped me grow up and become a man: my beloved late father, Paul P. Magada; my brother, Paul J. Magada; my mentor, Lt. Joseph A. Giampietro; and my friend, James N. DiPillo.

To my staff at Flying HIGH, Inc., who stand with me in my passion to meet the needs of people and change communities throughout the world.

To the many others who have helped me—you know who you are.

To the Lord Jesus Christ, my reason for living.

Thank you!

Endorsements

I want to encourage you to pick this book up and read it, because when you do you'll find yourself picking it up again and again. Jeff has taken the practical and powerful portions of a personal relationship with God and penned an excellent resource for "living the good life." It is God's desire and perfect will for each of us to live this life, and I pray that you will move into that fullness because of this writing.

Patrick McBane, executive director
Marketplace Solutions, Inc.

I have known Jeff Magada for over 20 years. Our paths have crossed on many occasions in ministry helping troubled youth and adults. Jeff's words of wisdom in this book are a road map to the practical application of life's teachings. They carry an extensive amount of credibility, as these pages have been walked out by Jeff himself in the furnace of his own personal life. He is very passionate for all to know a personal God. His thoughts are provoking to all who will read this excellent book.

Pastor Kevin Rauch, director of operations
Ohio Valley Teen Challenge

Table of Contents

Introduction

For we are God's [own] handiwork (His workmanship), recreated in Christ Jesus, [born anew] that we may do those good works which God predestined (planned beforehand) for us [taking paths which He prepared ahead of time], that we should walk in them [living the good life which He prearranged and made ready for us to live].

—Ephesians 2:10 AMP

THE GOOD LIFE. It's promised to us in the Book of Ephesians. Born again or not, everyone wants to live it. The phrase itself generates thoughts of having the ability to do what we want, when we want, and how we want—as well as having the ability to bless others. Living the good life also implies healthy, happy families, wonderful vacations, great jobs and fulfilling careers, successful ministries and businesses, owning nice cars and houses, and having access to the best in technology.

The good life is portrayed everywhere. It is portrayed abundantly in movies and television shows. Images of it fill magazines and other literature. People sing of it in music, preachers proclaim the promise of it from pulpits, and people talk about it, dream about it, and give all they've got to live it. Individually, people want to look good, feel good, and *live good*, especially when they believe they are *doing good* for the Kingdom of God.

A few years ago, I found myself in hot pursuit of the good life. I was busy doing good inside and outside of my local church. I tithed, gave offerings, read my Bible daily, and prayed. I worked hard to do good deeds in my community; yet, living the good life was no closer to me at that point than when I first became a Christian. In fact, it was so far away from me that I couldn't even see it anymore.

I knew plenty of success formulas, but I couldn't get any of them to work for me. I listened to and studied the teachings of prosperity preachers, but I was still very broke and saw no provision. Things were not going well. I was stuck. I needed clarity. I couldn't seem to get "the good life" results.

After too much time of struggling financially, socially, and internally, I began to seek out where I went wrong. I dissected every aspect of my life personally and professionally and learned that I had left out the essential element to living the good life—the pursuit of God's perfect will.

Living the Good Life focuses on the principles, underlying attitudes, and lifestyle changes necessary to truly live the good life that God has specifically designed for each of us. In essence, it is about learning how to develop the desire and discipline needed to yield to our new nature in Christ so that we fulfill the perfect will of God for every facet of our lives. Is this book derived from a journey that I went on to get to where I am now? Yes, it is. But more importantly, it is a call for the purification and maturing of the Body of Christ to live in pure obedience to God.

This book is written for those who are:

- on the cutting edge of breakthrough but can't seem to break through;
- experiencing sporadic, little bursts of success but not the continuous, abundant flow expected;
- in business, and while you feel that your products and services are of value and you've priced them to be fair in the marketplace, you can't seem to turn a profit;
- in similar situations of lack.

Whatever your story, I share mine and the biblical truths that set me free from financial hardships, relationship trouble, and various other problems.

Use this book as a guide to help you discover your own personal path to the good life God has prearranged for you to experience and enjoy. It was purposely printed in a convenient size, so you can carry it with you and refer to it throughout the day. Think of it as your "war manual" that will help keep you in God's perfect will for your life.

Live good!
Jeffrey M. Magada

Prayer of Salvation and Rededication

FOR THOSE WHO HAVE NOT YET RECEIVED Jesus Christ as Lord and Savior, or who have but are not living in complete obedience to Him, I invite you to fully surrender yourself to Him right now. You don't have to try to get your life cleaned up before you come to Him. Jesus wants you to come to Him just as you are—He will do the cleaning up. You *need* Him, and He *wants* you. Open your heart wholly to Him before you read another word in this book.

Pray this prayer:

Heavenly Father, I come to You in the name of Jesus Christ, and I ask You to forgive me for my disobedience to You. I totally open myself to You, and I ask Jesus to come into my heart. I receive Him, and I receive Your perfect will for my life. I declare now that Jesus is Lord over my life. I will obey Him. I will please Him. I will allow Him to do all the good He desires through me. Thank You, Father, for receiving me. Thank You for loving me. And thank You for making me a citizen of Your Kingdom and giving me Your nature. Amen!

Therefore if any man be in Christ, ***he is a new creature:*** *old things are passed away; behold,* ***all things are become new*** (2 Cor. 5:17).

Congratulations! You are now born of God and a citizen of His Kingdom. Glory to God! You are not what you used to be, no matter how good, bad, or ugly you were. That is not you anymore. You are better. Your true nature has been restored, and your old, sinful, selfish nature has passed away. You now have the *true nature* God originally created man to have before Adam's willful disobedience.

You no longer have a sinful, destructive nature that is selfish and stubborn and desires to disobey God and His commands. As a matter of fact, *selfishness, stubbornness, and disobedience are now unnatural for you.* By receiving Jesus Christ, you became a new creature with a new nature, recreated by God Himself, and restored to His image and likeness.

As a new member of the Body of Christ, I encourage you to get a copy of the Bible to read daily and to refer to as you read this book. Most Bibles outline a daily reading schedule that will aid you in getting started. If you are not a member of a local church, seek out a Word-teaching church that will love you and help you grow and mature in your new life with God.

Your brother in Christ,
Jeffrey Magada

Chapter 1

The Not-So-Good Life

I WAS PRETTY SERIOUS with the Lord when I started Flying HIGH, Inc., in 1994, a pioneering, tax-exempt, community-service organization designed to develop the potential of young people and adults in Mahoning Valley, Ohio. After a successful career as a social worker for my local police department, I resigned in 2001 to run Flying HIGH on a full-time basis. Flying HIGH was an all volunteer-run organization until I assumed full-time operations. I saw much potential in it. We were well-established in our community because we had an impact on the lives of thousands of youths through our League of Champions programs.

During this time, some relatives of mine who had a background in education thought it would be a good idea to open a learning center for kids struggling with reading and math. They asked me to put it under the umbrella of Flying HIGH. I agreed, because I wanted the learning center to become a viable business for them.

The learning center commenced operations and produced positive outcomes with hundreds of kids; however, we couldn't make enough to pay the bills, let alone turn a profit. That troubled me immensely. Here I was, an experienced social worker and former supervisor and caseworker of a successful program that was named a model for the state of Ohio, but I could not turn the learning center into a successful business. My mistakes and lack of knowledge were taking us further and further away from viability.

The learning center was struggling so much financially that it drained monies from my personal funds as well as the other program ambitions of Flying HIGH. Not good! There was something wrong, but what?

I put the learning center under the umbrella of Flying HIGH, *not* because God specifically instructed me to do so, but because those involved were family members. I thought their livelihood was not going to be good if I didn't do everything in my power to make it successful. There was no way I was going to let them down.

It was an honorable gesture, and collectively, we were providing a good service to the community. Nevertheless, I learned Psalm 127:1, *"Except the Lord build the house, they labour in vain that build it,"* the hard way. In other words, if God doesn't give directions to do a thing, even a "good thing," it is out of order and outside of His perfect will. And those who are trying to do it will experience just that—a *trying* thing.

Was the learning center a good thing? Yes. Was it good for the community? Yes. Were there success stories and testimonials from the children we served? Yes. Was it God's perfect will for me and for Flying HIGH? Well…no. After many attempts to justify its existence, I finally had to admit, it was not God's perfect will for me. And that was the problem.

No Provision. No Profit. No Peace.

Here's how I began to know that the learning center was outside of God's perfect will. It was not profitable; it could not stand on its own two feet. Make a note of this: *if it is not sustaining itself by making a profit, it is not God's perfect will.*

People don't want to hear a statement like that when they are in an unprofitable situation. Yet, that statement doesn't mean that what they are doing is a bad thing, or that all of what they are doing is out of God's will. Perhaps it's not for them to do in its entirety. Maybe there is simply an element of what they're doing that is outside of God's will, or there is only a certain part He wants them to do. When we as believers find out that our "good work" is unprofitable, our job is to find out from God what that part is.

In my case, Flying HIGH as a whole was in God's perfect will for me. The learning center, an element I had added to Flying HIGH, was not. There were others with tutoring services in the community that were successful and profitable. Ours, on the other hand was not meeting the business's needs, nor our needs, and consequently would not be there to meet the long-term needs of the community. The endeavor could prosper in someone else's hands. In itself, the learning center was not a bad thing; it was just not His perfect will for me.

Psalm 1:3 states, *"And he shall be like a tree planted by the rivers of water, that bringeth forth his fruit in his season; his leaf also shall not wither; and whatsoever he doeth shall prosper."* The key to that verse is the word *planted.* Who does the planting, the tree or the gardener? Where God plants, there is growth, and whatsoever the tree does there, where God has planted it, will prosper.

God's Process

Perhaps you are thinking, "Jeff, the learning center was a nonprofit organization. What do you mean, if it's not making a profit, it's not God's perfect will?"

Here's what I mean. It is the process that God showed me by which He accomplishes His works in the earth. This is also how He will direct you to do His work and how you will know that it is His will for you to do so. The direction and execution will be in this order:

- Step 1: The Vision or the Plan
- Step 2: The Provision
- Step 3: The Programming

Step 1: God will give you a vision or idea through time spent with Him and sometimes through personal experiences (see Joel 2:28). He then expects you to think and write out a plan, with His guidance, for how to implement this vision. For example, if God shows you a vision for a ministry or business, He is expecting a careful thinking through and consultation with Him for things such as,

- What is to be accomplished?
- What steps will get you there?
- What activities are involved with the steps?
- Who can you collaborate with (partners)?
- What are the necessary resources (people, equipment, materials, and facilities)?

Step 2: God expects you to do the necessary work to identify the provision that He has already prepared to fund the project (see Prov. 28:19). Once you have found the provision, He expects you to meet any requirements necessary to access and be a good steward of it.

Step 3: Finally, God expects program implementation along with the securing of proper funding. The funding empowers you to obtain staffing, facilities, licenses, supplies, equipment, and other necessary elements.

Consider the creation of man. Before God created man physically in Adam and placed him on the earth, the garden was prepared. The garden had the ability to replenish itself—be self-sustaining (see Gen. 1:11-12). Mankind, as well as every other living creature, was created with the ability to sustain their kind on the earth. God's vision comes with provision for sustainability, increase, and multiplication—in other words, profit. When God called Abram to leave the land of his fathers, Abram increased in cattle, land, and servants. God's provision was there for Abram to become Abraham, the father of many nations.

Profit is a part of the provision God uses to sustain the life of the vision and multiply the program. Every living thing has the ability to be fruitful and multiply itself. Profit helps a business, ministry, church, organization, outreach, and mission continue to fund itself and produce more and more fruit, thus multiplying its good results.

The phrase "where God guides, He provides" is true. Unfortunately, if we do not seek and yield to His guidance, we lack provision for where we are going, what we are doing, and those with whom we are attempting to build relationships. Lack of provision is a major indicator that God has not directed a ministry or business for the current time. You must know that God has directed it if you are going to put your faith to work and expect Him to provide for it. Consequently, when the provision is not there, but a determination to make it work is, desperation, for money in particular, sets in.

Beware of Pride and Ego

I know this desperation from firsthand experience and from observing others. I was full of fear. We were behind on bills, and debts kept mounting up. We were paralyzed. Without the Lord leading, I didn't have the financial, mental, emotional, or physical strength to make progress. I had become distracted by the obligations made to my family. I was not focused on what God wanted. All I could do was try to keep my obligations above water—try to keep them afloat. My loyalty to my family was greater than my loyalty to God.

In addition to a lack of *external* provision, I could also tell that I was outside of the will of God by the change in my *internal* character. When I became desperate for money, I stopped caring about people and started looking at them for what they could do for me. Business dealings were motivated by the desperation for money; I couldn't let the business go down. My attitude, perspective, thinking, and motivation were focused primarily on self-preservation.

My involvement was almost like a gambling addiction—I had to win; therefore, I kept putting more and more of my personal money on the table, along with monies from friends and acquaintances and business loans. However, none of it helped. Financially, we were just not making it.

I got caught up in pride and ego. I couldn't let the learning center fail. I wouldn't admit that it was not successful, that it was failing and needed to be shut down. I couldn't; my name was attached to it! I lived in a relatively small community, and if I admitted that it failed, it would appear that I failed and everyone would know. Even though Flying HIGH was doing other good things, the learning center was the retail arm. It was out in front, in the public eye, and highly visible. People saw it, so it became the most important to me. My attitude was, "If it goes down, I'm going down with it." And I did.

Make a note: pride and ego won't quit until you've hit rock bottom. Pride and ego will cause you to drain all of your personal resources. They will suck the zeal right out of you. Because I yielded to pride and ego, I learned what it is to be poor, down, and out. No matter how much I tried, tithed, and prayed—I was still broke. I felt sick; I was depressed. Every day was a repeat of the day before and the day before that and the month before that. Collectors were calling, dreams were fading, relationships became trying, and every combination or formula of success I applied still summed up to zero.

Still, I just kept struggling and trying and trying because "If at first, second, thirty-fifth you don't succeed, try and try again," right? The only difference is that all my trying didn't get me any closer to the goal. Instead, it led me further away and deeper into trouble. I wasn't learning or building from the previous attempts; I wasn't one step closer. Thomas Edison's story about the hundreds of times he failed before succeeding and my story were miles apart. All because I was trying to do something that was outside the perfect will of God.

Money Pressure Muddles Motives

People are not in their right minds when they have money pressure on them. I've observed preachers and ministers, specifically, under financial pressure who purposely posture themselves beside those who have money, only because of what they can do for their ministry or church. They don't know it, but to others they appear so needy! I can now see how God sees them: courting relationships under the influence of fear. Fear does what too much alcohol does to a person's motor skills; it distorts, blinds, and blurs. Fear will control a person's thinking, decisions, and actions if allowed.

Fear also distorts thinking regarding social positions and titles. I call it status deception. People can have the title of pastor, executive director, reverend, councilman, board member, or grand poobah but have no substance. They look good out there doing their thing, passing out business cards, giving elevator networking pitches, but they lack the true ability to carry out their assumed role or to change things and make a difference. In essence, they are perpetrating a lie. They personify Second Timothy 3:5, having only a form of godliness but no power. They have the title, but they have no power. They have a vision but no provision to bring it to pass. And if someone asks them to help fund another good work in the community, they would have nothing financially to give. I know. I've been there and done that.

Here's a check for examining relationships as they relate to growing a ministry or business. If you had the financial strength that you needed, meaning you could pay bills on time, debts are under control or paid off, you can purchase whatever is needed when it's needed, and there is money in savings and/or investments, would you be hanging on to the relationships you are currently in? If the answer is, "No, I would not be in those relationships," then it's time for a change.

You've Got to Want and Submit to God's Perfect Will

I shut the down the learning center in 2005. I walked into the office one day, and I said, "That's it. We will shut down in March." We notified all clients and quietly began phasing out the business.

The Lord did not force this decision on me. He waited to see what I was going to do. I had to choose to go after Him at the cost of everything, including the welfare of my relatives, my ego, and the price I would have to pay to correct things.

Peace started that day—peace, I should say, in the midst of a storm. Although the doors were closed, phasing out the business still required a lot of work on my part. We had incurred major debt and had back rent to pay for the space. I was bombarded with phone calls from collectors and vendors stopping in to see me and inquire about payment on our accounts. I was getting beat up mentally and emotionally from the stress and pressure to pay bills and pay off debts. Yet, the Lord kept all those "roaring lions" at bay.

It took some time, but we did it. We paid every debt, every penny we owed, including fines. The Lord's mercy truly does endure forever. He preserved our good name.

A while after we shut down the learning center and things began to turn around, I asked the Lord, "Why didn't You tell me?" The response I got almost seemed apologetic: "I couldn't tell you because you weren't willing to do it, and if I did tell you, it would have hardened your heart." God was so right. My attitude and thinking were so focused on what I thought was right that if He had blatantly told me to shut down the learning center, or not open it at all, I would have become even more determined to stay where I was and do things my way. I certainly would not have offered God lifted hands and shouts of praise at the sound of "Shut down the learning center; It's not My will for you."

Every argument and justification I could think of would have come forth: "It's doing a good thing! It's a good work! Don't You want us to be about doing good? People are depending on me. What about my family and their welfare? God would not instruct me to do such a thing! This must be the voice of the devil disguised as God's voice to take out my good name in the community and sabotage the organization's future success. No, I will not shut it down! We will press toward the mark of the prize of the high calling!"

How stupid I had been to stay there so long! I was nowhere near "the high calling." In fact, I was moving further and further away from the high calling, His perfect will, and consequently hindering the good life He had for me, my family members, and those in the community we served.

Your Turn: Turn a Not-So-Good Life Around

Have you ever found yourself in situations where you wish God would just show up, knock on your door, and blatantly tell you exactly what you need to do that would turn your situation around? How many times do you long for that *one word from God* that could change your whole life?

Perhaps an impending hard heart is why He doesn't do so. Why give someone direction if he is not going to follow it? Why provide a person with wisdom if all he is going to do is become more determined to follow through with what he *wants* to be *the right thing* to do? That's throwing pearls of wisdom before swine. It's not valued; it will just get trampled on while he is on his way to the slop he considers more precious. Let's be real. God already knows that there are times when *we don't want to hear what He has to say!*

I shared my story. What's yours? Is it very different from mine? Is there a situation in your life, ministry, or business you desire to turn around? Are you ready to hear that one word from God that will change things? Are you ready to live the good life? Here are a couple of action steps to take to turn a not-so-good life around.

Action Points

1. Consider your own story. Are there any "unprofitable" situations that you just can't seem to figure out?

   A. If so, share those with God and ask Him to reveal to you where a change is needed. Simply give Him permission to help you in every area of your life. (See Proverbs 3:5-6; Isaiah 55:8-11; Matthew 6:24-33.)

   B. If not, ask God to show you areas where He desires to lead you more in fulfilling His perfect will for you in what you do.

2. Be open to living God's perfect will for you. You have to accept it and trust God. Do it in faith. Say this aloud: "I

accept and receive God's perfect will for every area of my life."

These two steps will be the foundation for receiving and applying the remaining lessons of this book.

The Not-So-Good Life Study Guide

Study to shew thyself approved unto God, a workman that needeth not to be ashamed, rightly dividing the word of truth.

—2 Timothy 2:15

1. **Define the Good Life**

   A. Ephesians 2:10, "*...[taking paths which He prepared ahead of time], that we should walk in them [living the good life which He prearranged and made ready for us to live]*" (AMP).

2. **Psalm 127:1,** "*Except the Lord build the house...*"

3. **God's Perfect Will Is Profitable**

   A. Psalm 1:3, "*...he shall be like a tree planted by the rivers of water...*"

B. The Plan—God gives the vision or idea

C. The Provision—Identify the places of God's provision

D. The Programming—Execute when the plan and provision are in place

4. **Beware of Pride and Ego**

A. Proverbs 16:18, "*Pride goeth before destruction...*"

B. 1 John 2:16, "*...and the pride of life, is not of the Father...*"

5. **Money Pressure Muddles Motives**

A. 1 Timothy 6:10, "*For the love of money is the root of all evil...*"

B. Matthew 6:24, "*No man can serve two masters...*"

6. **Submit to God's Perfect Will**

A. Romans 12:2, "*...be not conformed to this world...*

B. Colossians 4:12, "*...stand perfect and complete in all the will of God.*"

7. **Turn a Not-So-Good-Life Around**

A. Seek God's direction for where change is needed in your life.

B. Proverbs 3:5-6, "*Trust in the Lord…in all thy ways acknowledge Him…*"

C. Isaiah 55:8-11, "*…for My thoughts are not your thoughts…*"

D. Matthew 6:24-33, "*No man can serve two masters….seek ye first the kingdom of God…*"

Notes

Notes

Chapter 2

Clean Up Your ACT: Alliances, Connections, and Ties

NOW THAT WE'VE ASKED GOD to reveal to us where change is needed in our lives and we are willing to follow His perfect will for our lives, let's talk about relationships. Relationships are crucial to fulfilling the work God desires for us to do. It was my attitude toward certain relationships that got me out of the will of God. Relationships kept me from hearing God properly and doing what He said to do. Relationships made me fearful and distrustful. If you are not fully obeying God, chances are someone else is involved, and your relationship with him or her is aiding your willful disobedience.

Alliances Will Make You or Break You

An alliance is *a close association for a common objective.*[1] Who do you have close to you and why? There may be many justifiable reasons. However, the only reason that matters is if those relationships are God's perfect will for your life.

Let's take a look at some biblical alliances. David and Bathsheba: Would David have had an affair with her if he had been honoring God in his relationships (see 2 Sam. 11)? Samson and Delilah: Would Samson have allowed himself to love Delilah if he knew he would have his eyes gouged out and be bound with chains (see Judg. 16)? David and Saul: Would David have been King Saul's attendant if he knew King Saul would attempt to kill him, especially when God never called David to attend to King Saul (see 1 Sam. 16:18-23; 18:1-16)? God called David to be king. Last, Moses and his brother Aaron: While Moses was up on the mountain receiving God's instructions to help His people, Aaron was feeding their rebellion against God by helping them make a golden calf (see Exod. 32). Wasn't Aaron only with Moses because of Moses's insecurity with speaking (see Exod. 4:14)? God did not initiate any of these alliances.

The bottom line is that none of these people would have entered into these relationships if they would have obeyed God. That's why God says in First Corinthians 15:33 (NASB), *"Do not be deceived: 'Bad company corrupts good morals.'"* There are people deceived right now because they are involved in unhealthy relationships and alliances with others. They don't even realize that these relationships are having a negative effect on everything in their lives: finances, health, work, marriage, children, and most of all, their relationship with God. They just can't seem to figure out why things are not working out and how they got themselves into such a mess. Although they are trying very hard, things are just not working successfully.

Character Flaws

When I was desperately trying to keep the learning center afloat, I formed alliances with many who influenced my behavior. Their character flaws became a part of me because we were connected. My character started changing. Because I cared more about preserving myself, my ego, and my pride, and keeping the business from failing, I didn't have time for the financially "ordinary" folks. If I thought a relationship would lead to a potential money resource, I catered to developing it. If I thought a person couldn't help me, I put that relationship on hold. Creating these unhealthy alliances bothered my conscience, but I ignored that, and I ignored God's instructions in Romans 12:16: *"Live in harmony with each other. Don't be too proud to enjoy the company of ordinary people. And don't think you know it all!"* (see Rom. 12:16 NLT). I reasoned that my involvement in those relationships was only temporary, and that they were for a good cause—for the kids in the community.

Seeking Human Validation

With the business struggling and my personal finances in bad shape, my self-esteem plummeted to zero. Not only was I financially needy, but I was emotionally needy as well and sought for some type of relief. I needed validation. I needed confirmation from someone that what I was doing was a "good" thing. I needed someone to tell me that I was "OK."

Instead of turning to God, I turned to the comfort of a woman in ways I should not have. I knew that I was not supposed to be in that relationship, but I had become so needy for human approval that I couldn't seem to cut it off. It wasn't until I cut off the business that I gained the strength to end that relationship as well.

Can you see how one decision outside of the will of God gave birth to more and more decisions outside of God's will? However, when the root was exposed and corrected, the other branches of bad decisions easily wilted.

We cannot play around with being outside the will of God. The worse a situation gets, the more wrong decisions will be made, the more poor alliances will be formed, and the more the struggle to make something "good" happen intensifies. Yet, all of these attempts will continue to yield nothing.

When people feel bad about themselves, they follow a path that leads to fear of rejection, and next they find themselves dealing with approval addiction. They will look for approval from anywhere and anyone: career status, colleagues, the community, parents, and new relationships—even morally wrong ones. If validation expected from one relationship doesn't happen, they frequently move on to another and another, seeking approval and acceptance. God's validation of who we are and what we are doing is not enough for those caught in this cycle. When He does not validate what we are doing, it's a telltale sign that we're on the wrong path.

Let Go of Strongholds

I was raised in an Italian home. Italians possess very strong cultural bonds and family ties. We are taught to take care of our family at any cost, a noble and honorable tradition, but not at the expense of God's will. When I got involved with my family members' desire to open the learning center, my initial purpose was to make sure that "the family" was successful with a viable business. I was successful in my other endeavors, so I thought it was only right that I get involved. When I made the decision to shut down the learning center, the reaction of the family members involved was primarily one of relief. We were struggling anyway. They simply accepted the decision and prepared to move on. Conversely, I had family members outside of the situation giving me the "evil eye." They gave me the "how-dare-you-let-the-family-down-like-this" look.

I learned the meaning behind what God spoke to Abram in Genesis 12:1 when He instructed him to get away from his country, kinfolk, and father's house, and what Jesus said in Matthew 10:37, "*He that loveth father or mother more than Me is not worthy of Me: and he that loveth son or daughter more than me is not worthy of Me.*" Basically, God is saying that if you are more committed to fulfilling your family's will than His, you have an obedience issue. God has no tolerance for that. Despite strong family relationships, I had to choose to follow God's will, and that meant shutting down the learning center, even at the risk of turning my back on my cultural values and making "family enemies."

It takes breaking through cultural norms to walk in God's perfect will. In the movie *The Godfather III*, the cousin, the right-hand man, is dating the leader's daughter, and they are madly in love—like Romeo and Juliet. At one point in the movie, the leader tells him to end the relationship with his daughter. The cousin goes to the girl (or his love) and basically says, "It's over." Just like that. No questions, no explanations, simply, "It's over." What the leader commanded had a higher priority than his desires and his love for the girl. If the world can do it, how much more should we as Christians be able to? *If a person cannot break away from his culture to do God's will, he will be limited the rest of his life.* Being devoted more to our cultural norm than to God's Word positions us to experience Mark 7:13, *"Making the word of God of none effect through your tradition, which ye have delivered: and many such like things do ye."*

Since gaining a revelation of Matthew 10:37, I will end a relationship in seconds, whether personal, business, or professional—it doesn't matter what type. If God says no, the relationship has to go. I have simply made my loyalty to God stronger than my loyalty to any human being. He has taught me to be loyal to Him no matter what the cost.

As a rule, I consider these two factors when aligning my life with the perfect will of God.

1. If it's a business venture and it's not profitable, I end it.
2. If it's a person I'm connecting with and I gather that *he or she is not thinking like me and not talking like me*, the connection does not continue.

The latter is not to say that I do not value diversity and inclusion. Nor is it saying that I am not loyal to my relationships. As a matter of fact, I am more loyal now to love others more than ever because I'm more loyal to God's commandment to do so. I appreciate and understand the value of evaluating relationships in fulfilling God's will, purposes, and plans. The latter refers to being of like mind in vision, mission, purpose, character, and purity of motive.

Once I got this principle, I lost interest in impressing other people and proving myself. My only focus now is to do what God tells me to do. No more, no less. When I'm in business meetings, my goal is to do no more than what God wants me to do—popular or unpopular. My standards are *did it please God,* and *did it help Him accomplish His purposes?* We must lock into this type of thinking.

Identify any controlling negative influences over yourself and sever them. Otherwise you will constantly be faced with their intimidation, leading you in a direction away from God's perfect will.

Beware of Negative Influences

No matter what I did, it was never good enough because inferiority was present. Therefore, I never fully liked myself. I was constantly trying to do things to please people—to keep connections with people that gave me a sense of being good enough. When they were pleased, when they cheered, when they gave me a pat on the back, the inferiority complex was satisfied for the moment. In my younger days, I was an athlete and was very performance-driven. I thought when I performed well that I was good and when I performed badly that I was bad. I didn't know that "I" was not my performance.

I also didn't know how strong an influence inferiority was until the business began to fail. Failing for a secure person is just that—something isn't working, so the person has to do something to fix it or do something else. To people who are insecure in their self-worth, failing is a word that means there is something wrong with them. They believe they are not good enough to succeed at this, but if they don't succeed at it, other people will find out how worthless they really are. Insecure people can't have that, so they believe they have to do something. The drama grows from there.

I discovered that inferiority was a generational issue hidden deep within my makeup. My good intentions to keep the business running and make it viable were secretly married to the need to measure up, to do something that the family would esteem highly. I was saving the business for the wrong motive.

I was trying to validate myself and others, with little thought for pleasing God.

When I finally realized how inferiority had influenced me and controlled my thoughts, decisions, and actions, I immediately repented and asked God to heal me inside. He responded by supernaturally removing my need to validate or prove myself by giving me a revelation of His great love for me. I responded to His great love for me by changing my attitude. It was now one of "I hear and do, because I love You." My love for God was my motivation. How could I please Him? How could I help Him? How could I advance His Kingdom, plans, and purposes?

People have different influences imbedded within their makeup. When people discover that something has been misguiding them, it's an awakening and enlightening moment. Those who truly desire to purify their hearts will take time in the presence of God to uncover and overcome the thing that has been misguiding them. Others will know that it's there but won't deal with it. They don't want to bring any related deep wounds, hurts, or depressions to the surface. So instead, they continue to cover it up and stay victims of shame, embarrassment, and the pressure to perform.

Clean Up Your ACT: Alliances, Connections, and Ties

If my story resembles yours in any way, I advise you to do as I did and obey the Lord Jesus Christ and cut off those relationships that are hindering His progress in your life. Do it now! They are cutting you off from the power of God working in your life and stopping you from fulfilling His perfect will. I believe God is speaking to you right now. He is revealing what relationships you need to cut off. It makes no difference how involved you are with these relationships. Don't be afraid. Cut them off! Whether a business or personal relationship, do not seek what is convenient and comfortable. Rather, seek God's perfect will for your life.

While we're cutting away what and who does not belong, let's get rid of immorality as well. Whether it's fornication (sex outside of marriage) or adultery (sex with someone to whom you are not married), it is disobedience to God. Stealing, lying, and deceiving others is blatant disobedience to God. If you are connected to any of these types of behaviors, decide to stop right now! When you cut these relationships and behaviors from your life, *you will cut off all control they have over you.*

Separate Yourself

Cutting off relationships, even those within one's own family, in order to live the good life that God has predestined for us to live is by no means out of the ordinary. God directed Abraham to leave his country, his relatives, and his father's house. Why? So he could pursue God's perfect will for his life and so that, consequently, "*...in him all the families of the earth would be blessed*" (see Gen. 12:1-3). Did this happen? It sure did. Through Abraham's seed came Jesus Christ (see Gal. 3:16).

God separated Abraham so He could start the restoration plan for man, which eventually culminated in Christ Jesus.

It seems that God uses separation to accomplish restoration in our lives. While on earth, He wants us to live an abundant life in His kingdom and experience all of its advantages, just as Adam did before his rebellion/willful disobedience. *Therefore, He separates us from all that would keep us separated from Him and prevent us from partaking of all He has provided for us.* God desires to keep us from sin (anything that blocks His power from operating in our lives) and death (that which disconnects us from pure fellowship with Him). In other words, separation is God's way of restoring His abundant life—His perfect will—to our lives. He's not trying to take things or people from you to make you miserable or lonely. God separates to give us something greater (see James 4:6), not so we experience loss. Settle this truth in your heart: *God's perfect will for your life will always be to your advantage, the advantage of others, and the advancement of the Kingdom of God on the earth. God's perfect will for your life is the fulfillment of your ultimate destiny and highest potential.*

Separation may be physically relocating, like Abraham; it may be totally cutting off all communication or association with a person or thing; or it may be simply disconnecting from a way of thinking and decision making. Separating from family is a prime example of the latter. While you may still visit with Uncle Lou at the Thanksgiving dinner celebration and might even have to keep the lines of communication open because he's taking care of your grandmother, you don't have to operate or live by Uncle Lou's principles and thought-processes that are contrary to how God desires you to think and operate.

All throughout the Bible you will see God separating His people from things and people to move them into His abundant life (perfect will). He separates us from the world and unto Himself to accomplish His abundant life (perfect will) in our lives so we can be blessed and be a blessing to the world. God calls this separated state *sanctification* or *holiness.*

> *So you must live as God's obedient children. Don't slip back into your old ways of living to satisfy your own desires. You didn't know any better then. But now you must be holy in everything you do, just as God who chose you is holy. For the Scriptures say, "You must be holy because I am holy."* (1 Pet. 1:14-16 NLT).

Holiness comes from its root word *holy.* Holy means "pure and without ulterior motive; separated, and set apart from any and all evil."[2] When God says, *"You must be holy,"* He is instructing you about the condition in which He wants you to keep your heart. He is not referring to your outward appearance. *Holiness is an inward desire to please God and walk in His perfect will for your life,* so that through your abundant life others can also be blessed and experience all the advantages of living in the Kingdom of God. Holiness is seeing eye-to-eye with God and making His desires your desires, His plans your plans, and His will your will. Holiness is having a pure heart. Your heart literally becomes a reflection (image) of His heart, and you are willing to separate yourself from anything or anyone that is not in His perfect will for your life.

Look for the Fruit

I had become so focused on having people like me that my senses were untrained, and I was vulnerable. When I began to refocus on what God would have me do and with whom He'd have me connect, I had to retrain my senses.

After the close of the learning center, I regrouped, prayed, and started hiring staff members again. I met a lady who was a believer and always wanted to do our type of work. I went through the process of interviewing her and eventually hiring her. During her first week, we went to a typical two-hour meeting. I looked over, and her eyes were closed! This was her *first* meeting, during her *first* week! That was it. She was released the next day.

That experience showed me something. Even with all the conversations we may have with people, we can still be vulnerable to making mistakes (and this can be tough with Christian people because they have the lingo down). While our senses are in training, we can look at the apparent fruit—the behavior, results, and attitudes of a person—to discern who is to be in relationship with us. I tell my staff I am not obligated to anyone. I know God is going to tell me to do things that other people are not going to agree with, and I'll get some arguments against it. He's not concerned with that. He wants to get done what He wants to get done.

After firing the lady, I asked the Lord why this happened. He responded by asking me, "Did you believe me for her? Was your faith pulling her in, or did you just get to know her and bring her on board?" It was a lesson in learning to seek God's perfect will, even in the course of decisions we feel capable of making and have been successful at making in the past. To walk in God's perfect will takes utilizing your faith constantly. From that moment on, I used my faith to connect with the right people. I simply ask God to bring the right people, and I believe I receive them according to Mark 11:24.

In business partnerships, it's important to consider why we choose to go into business with the partners we are with. Is it because we've known them for along time, or is it because they are qualified? A great business plan can be jeopardized greatly if the partners' ways of thinking are not in alignment and working together with yours.

Allow God's Wisdom to Guide You in All Relationships

From this point on, I encourage you to never pursue a relationship or alliance with anyone without asking God for His wisdom to guide you. He knows exactly where people ought to be in your life at certain times and whether it's healthy for you to be close to them or if you need to keep them at arm's length.

He will clearly reveal this to you. Not everybody is meant to have the same type of relationship with you. God will show you who to pursue a close relationship with, who to have as acquaintances, and who to keep out of your life. Follow God's leading in *all* relationships.

Along with God's wisdom to guide you, also ask Him to give you an understanding and wise heart. (Solomon prayed for this in First Kings 3:9.) An understanding and wise heart is the ability to discern people's motives and intentions. The dictionary defines the word *discern* as "to perceive or recognize, make out clearly."[3] How important is it to God that you have this ability to perceive, recognize, and make out clearly people's motives and intentions? It is so important that He instructs you to go into training to develop it, just as a baseball player would go into spring training before the season. Let's see what God says in Hebrews 5:14 about "senses training": *"But solid food is for the mature, who because of practice have their senses trained to discern good and evil"* (NASB).

God wants you to practice distinguishing the good and evil in people. *He wants you to watch what they do and listen to what they say.* He wants you to have your eyes and ears wide open so you can recognize people's motives and intentions immediately. *Don't like someone simply because he or she likes you.* That kind of thinking is childish and selfish. God wants you to train yourself to see people as they are and not to allow yourself to be blinded by your own insecurities. Remember the mess Moses got himself into with his brother Aaron. You no longer are in desperate need for people to accept you. As a born-again believer, you have a new nature that is *"...made full and having come to fullness of life..."* (Col. 2:10 AMP). As a new creature in Christ Jesus, your nature is not half full—you are full and come to fullness of life in your relationship with God. *Look to Him for your acceptance and recognition.* He will fulfill you much, much, much more than any human being can! He longs for you to do this.

Connect With Pure-Hearted People

God wants you to develop healthy, vibrant relationships. He even instructs you who to have them with in Second Timothy 2:22 (NASB): *"Now flee from youthful lusts, and pursue righteousness, faith, love, and peace, with those who call on the Lord from a pure heart."* Did you see it? *"...those who call on the Lord from a pure heart."* God wants you connected with pure-hearted people. You may be asking, "Where do I find these pure-hearted people?" This answer is simple. These people will be found as you pursue God's perfect will for your life and use your faith to pull them in.

As you pursue His perfect will for your life, you allow Him to form a "pure heart" in you: *"But the goal of our instruction is love from a pure heart and a good conscience and a sincere faith"* (1 Tim. 1:5 NASB). He works on forming this in you so you are able to have a healthy, vibrant relationship with Him. Remember what Jesus said in Matthew 5:8: *"Blessed are the pure in heart, for they shall see God"* (NASB). A pure heart is the prerequisite to a healthy, vibrant relationship with God and others. Why? There is no selfishness in a pure heart. Pure-hearted people want to serve others by giving to them, and they want to receive what others have to give.

This is why God works a "pure heart" in us (see Titus 2:14). He wants us able to receive all His love and in turn, be able to give love back to Him and others. He wants us to give love to Him by obeying His instructions and by doing the things that please Him (see 1 John 5:3) because the better we are at giving to Him, the better we will be at receiving from Him. *Wow!* Isn't that something? *God wants to form a "pure heart" in us so we can receive all that He desires to give and so we can have healthy, vibrant relationships with others, to the fullest.* I would say God knows what He's doing, and He has this relationship thing all figured out.

Can you now see why God wants to connect you closely with people who are allowing Him to actively accomplish the same goal in their lives? God wants you linked with kindred spirits who also *"press on toward the goal for the prize of the upward call of God in Christ Jesus"* (Phil. 3:14 NASB). These are the people who will put the most into their relationship with you. Just like you, God has worked out the selfishness in them, and they have become good at giving and receiving. They yearn to please God; they yearn also to have close relationships with others. About them God says, "These are My children who are pleasing to Me; go ahead and have a pleasing relationship with them."

The good news is you don't have to rush into finding these "pure" relationships. In due season, God will provide them as you pursue His perfect will. The apostle Paul referred to some frustration in this very area as he commended Timothy to the Philippians: *"For I have no one else of kindred spirit who will genuinely be concerned for your welfare. For they all seek after their own interests, not those of Christ Jesus"* (Phil. 2:20-21 NASB). With these words, Paul gives us valuable insight regarding the signs of pure-hearted people. *They are genuinely concerned for the welfare of others, and they seek the interests of Jesus Christ and His Kingdom.* This makes sense because there is no selfishness in them, and their attention is always on advancing the interests of the Kingdom of God, and the welfare of others. *Therefore, your relationship with a pure-hearted person will not result in you compromising yourself in any way, because self-gratification is no longer their main interest. These people want you to be more of who you are and who God has called you to be.*

Jesus found His close relationships and divine connections as He was simply going along pursuing God's perfect will for His life, and so will you. John chapter 1 records the account of how Jesus found His disciples. I encourage you to take some time and study how He did so. Take special note of what Jesus said to Nathaniel in John 1:47: *"Behold an Israelite indeed, in whom is no guile!"* Now how did Jesus know that there was *"no guile"* (deceit) in Nathaniel? Because He used His divine powers as the Son of God? Not necessarily. I believe it was because He had developed an understanding and wise heart (see Luke 2:40, 52; Isa. 11:2), just like God is working in each of us.

Train your senses to know the heart and motives of people. Just because you are good with people in one area of your life—socially, for example—doesn't mean that you will be good in other areas. As you train yourself in that regard, you will learn where people need to be in your life and where you need to be in theirs.

Action Points

In cleaning up your ACT, ask God

- For His wisdom to guide you in all relationships (a good prayer is found in Philippians 1:9-11).
- To give you an understanding and wise heart.
- To give you relationships that are in His perfect will for your life, relationships with pure-hearted people that are divine connections appointed only by Him.

Endnotes

1. Webster's New World Dictionary, 2nd College Edition, s.v., "alliance."

2. Myles Munroe, *Rediscovering the Kingdom* (Shippensburg, PA: Destiny Image Publishers, 2004), 157-8.

3. See http://www.yourdictionary.com/discern.

Clean Up Your ACT: Alliances, Connections, and Ties Study Guide

Study to shew thyself approved unto God, a workman that needeth not to be ashamed, rightly dividing the word of truth.

—2 Timothy 2:15

1. **1 Corinthians 15:33**, "*...evil communications corrupt good manners.*"
2. **Alliances Will Make You or Break You**
3. **Character Flaws**
4. **Seeking Human Validation**
5. **Letting Go of Strongholds**

A. Matthew 10:37, *"...He that loveth father or mother more than Me is not worthy of Me..."*

B. Mark 7:9, *"...ye reject the commandment of God, that ye may keep your own tradition."*

C. Mark 7:13, *"Making the word of God of none effect through your tradition..."*

6. **Negative Influences**

A. Jeremiah 17:5, *"...Cursed be the man that trusteth in man..."*

B. Deuteronomy 28:13, *"...the Lord shall make thee the head, and not the tail..."*

7. **Cut Off Hindering Relationships** (Clean Up Your ACT: Alliances, Connections, and Ties)

8. **Allow God's Wisdom to Guide You in All Relationships**

A. 1 Kings 3:9, *"Give therefore thy servant an understanding heart to judge thy people..."*

B. Hebrews 5:14, *"...those who by reason of use have their senses exercised to discern both good and evil."*

9. **Look for the Fruit of Character**

A. Matthew 12:33, *"...for the tree is known by his fruit..."*

B. Matthew 12:34, *"...for out of the abundance of the heart the mouth speaketh."*

C. Luke 6:45, *"A good man out of the good treasure of his heart bringeth forth that which is good..."*

10. Connect With Pure-hearted People

A. 2 Timothy 2:22, *"...with those who call on the Lord from a pure heart"* (NASB).

B. 1 Timothy 1:5, *"...charity out of a pure heart, and of a good conscience..."*

C. Philippians 2:20-21 *"...For I have no man likeminded...For all seek their own..."*

11. Jesus, Our Example

A. John 1:47, *"...Behold an Israelite indeed, in whom is no guile!"*

B. Luke 2:40, *"...and the grace of God was upon him."*

C. Luke 2:52, *"And Jesus increased in wisdom and stature..."*

D. Isaiah 11:2, *"...the spirit of wisdom and understanding..."*

12. Separate Yourself Unto the Lord

A. Genesis 12:1, *"...the LORD had said unto Abram, Get thee out of thy country, and from thy kindred..."*

B. 2 Corinthians 6:17, *"Wherefore come out from among them, and be ye separate..."*

C. James 4:6, *"...God resisteth the proud, but giveth grace unto the humble."*

D. 1 Peter 1:14-16, *"...as he which hath called you is holy, so be ye holy in all manner of conversation..."*

13. Pray for God's Help in Establishing Relationships

A. Philippians 1:9-11, *"...that your love may abound...in knowledge and in all judgment..."*

Notes

Notes

CHAPTER 3

A Willful Decision

THE STORIES I SHARE in this chapter are real-life examples of how all of what I've talked about so far was applied, and resulted in achieving God's perfect will. Warning: they are not all glamorous. I share them because they illustrate the need for guts and steadfastness to follow after God's heart regardless of opposition. I pray that they will bring clear understanding as to why we cannot be bound by people and relationships and allow them to take higher priority than God. I trust that you will see how God's power, His ability to change situations and circumstances, is connected to fulfilling His will. And more than anything, I desire for God to give you a hearing heart to hear what the Holy Spirit would speak to you concerning the perfect will of God for your individual lives.

God respects our decisions. Suppose Abraham disobeyed God and never separated himself from all he knew to pursue what and who God wanted him to know. Would he still have fulfilled God's perfect will for his life? No way! Here's why.

Everything God does and everything He instructs us to do has a purpose. That purpose is always tied to Him accomplishing His perfect will in our lives. If we choose not to obey God's perfect will for us, then He will allow us to live without Him and with the results of our choices. If Abraham would have chosen to selfishly disobey God's instruction and stayed where he was, he would have fulfilled his own will for his life instead of God's perfect will for him. God would have let him live with the results of his decision, just as He let Adam live with the consequences of his disobedient choice. God will always let us live with our choices because He will not violate the authority He gave us to control ourselves and our environment. That's why, to become a citizen of His Kingdom, we must choose to confess with our mouth, and believe in our heart (see Rom. 10:9-10). God gives us the final say-so, whether His perfect will is accomplished in our lives or not.

That's exactly what happened to me and the learning center experience. I was sure of what I was doing and what I thought was the way to go, and God respected the authority He gave me to live my life my way. While I could see the handwriting on the wall, so to speak, He did not force the closing of the center. There were times before when God would speak to me directly about what to do and what not to do. In this case, the Lord did not make the decision for me; He didn't say it directly. Instead, He waited to see what I was going to do.

The inward desire to please God and walk in His perfect will for your life begins with a willful decision. It's a decision to lay down your wants, desires, preferences, plans, and motives for God's.

To follow the instructions for God's perfect will, you have to be courageous. In Joshua, God instructs him to be strong and courageous: *"As I was with Moses, so I will I be with thee"* (Josh. 1:5). You can follow the life of Joshua and see that he perfectly obeyed God, and you can see accomplishment after accomplishment of the will of God through his obedient lifestyle.

Strength and courage don't just happen. There will be many distractions and adversaries pressing you to do what's comfortable, conforming, or convenient. Maturity is the key. Once you've made a decision to bind your will to the perfect will of God, you will continue to strengthen your capacity and ability to do so. Let me share a couple of examples.

On the Firing Line

The Lord spoke to me about nominating a person to serve on a particular public board on which I serve. The nomination caused a big hullabaloo. Some had made it clear that they did not want any more "faith-based" people on this board. So the battle began. Intimidation, haughtiness, cold shoulders, etc., all stood up to build a wall against my nomination. I was the only one promoting this person's participation on the board. The temptation to compromise my actions was strong. I wanted to reason with God. "Hey, God, I nominated him, but they don't want him. But I did what You told me to do, so…it's on You. I'm not going to say anything else about him." Instead I asked God, "What do You want me to do?" His response was, "What I commanded you to do." At my first mention of him to the board, he was not nominated. At my second mention of him, his nomination was turned down again. Well, guess what happened the third time that He was nominated? You got it. He was unanimously appointed to serve on the board. It took three tries and three years, but God commanded it, and I wasn't giving up on it until He gave me permission.

On a different occasion while serving on the same board, the distribution of hundreds of thousands of dollars to certain community service providers was up for discussion. One of these community service providers continued to receive funds, even though they were not managing their funds very well. God's instructions came for me to have nothing to do with mismanagement. The time came to approve very large monetary allocations to this provider. When the votes were counted, I had the only *no* vote. You can imagine the stares I got, but I stayed obedient. I simply stayed consistent in my *no* vote and expressed my concerns. Shortly afterward, mismanagement was officially discovered, and that provider had to shut down. Another agency took over their community services.

Three years prior to that time, I wouldn't have done any of these things. I would have refused to nominate another faith-based person to a board that I knew would oppose the idea, and I definitely would not have been the only man standing alone in a *no* vote to provide funds to a community service provider. Carrying out God's instructions can be difficult, because no one wants to be the "odd man out."

The $500,000 Fruit of Obedience

Recently, in my state, over a million dollars in funding was made available statewide for faith- and community-based organizations. Selecting recipients would be done on a competitive basis via a grant process.

In the past, I would have immediately asked, "How can *I* get this money to do something for the at-risk youth?" At-risk youth are the primary focus of Flying HIGH. The initiative would have been about what *I* think the best use of the money would have been. Then *I* would have zealously begun to put together a proposal and support that validated *my* thoughts.

Instead, I literally asked God, "What do You want this funding to be used for?" His response was, "Ex-offenders." Without question, I proceeded to think how God was thinking. Serving at-risk youths, the funding would be limited primarily to females between the ages of 16 and 21 who were involved in out-of-wedlock pregnancy. By serving ex-offenders, the funds could be used to serve the offender, his or her spouse, and their children of any age. There would be a larger opportunity for impacting the community by serving ex-offenders than there would be only focusing on at-risk youths. Serving ex-offenders would allow our organization to service our primary group and then some. God's thoughts were definitely higher than my thoughts.

A meeting of various faith- and community-based organizations was held to discuss which of the three areas to apply for. The funding could be used toward 1) healthy marriages, 2) at-risk youths, or 3) ex-offenders. During the meeting, all the talk was for applying for the money to serve the at-risk youth population. So I raised my hand to make the suggestion to go for ex-offenders. "Now Jeff," one of the leaders warned. "Don't be throwing us off." The atmosphere was definitely anti-Jeff Magada even before I began to speak. Nevertheless, I stood firm to promote the cause that God wanted to address. I made my suggestion, but it was not well received at all. In the eyes of just about everyone present, I was way off base. After much deliberation, a decision was made. Those who wanted to put together a grant for ex-offenders would get with me, and those who wanted to submit a grant for at-risk youths would get together.

Well, the ex-offender group was small—me and three others. We went to work putting together all the necessary narratives and documents needed for the grant proposal. We completed it through some excellent teamwork and submitted it on time. Well, the time came for the announcement of grant recipients. We got it! The small ex-offender focus group would receive more than $500,000 in funding over the next three years for our community. Flying HIGH would get a substantial portion to help ex-offenders *and* their at-risk kids.

The blessing came. It was hard work applying for it, but God instructed it. This is where the *spiritual* walk made a *physical* difference. Bottom line, God said, "Here's what I want the money used for." We made up our minds to follow through regardless of the reactions of people or unfavorable circumstances—even though we were few in number to complete the grant proposal. Once His instructions were obeyed, His power—His part in getting it done—showed up to get the grant approved. Can you see how God's profitable process worked here? The provision was there, more than $500,000; He gave the vision (use for serving ex-offenders); and the programming followed through my organization and the other organizations who worked with us to get the funding.

The at-risk youth group got no funding. Their response to our getting the funding was not congratulatory. The leader who rebuked me during the meeting was the only one who came to apologize for not listening.

Shortly thereafter, another funding opportunity came at a federal level to help bolster the capacity of faith- and community-based organizations. Only 100 organizations in the United States would receive the funding. Flying HIGH took the lead to put together a consortium to apply for the funding. The Lord spoke to me concerning who to include in that consortium, and the organization of that leader who rebuked me from the community meeting was one of those organizations. As anticipated, Flying HIGH and its consortium were among the 100 to receive funding. We received a very substantial amount of money again over a three-year period to benefit at-risk youths. *Wow!* Isn't God something! He has provision stored up in particular places for us. We just have to obey Him over what we think. He has more than enough for all He has assigned for us to do. We just need to be obedient and on time.

In the past, I would have never even asked God what to do about getting the funding, let alone what *He* wanted to do with the funding. He had worked that into my heart to ask when I totally began to pursue His perfect will. Before, I was too fearful to ask that question because I was needy. I was just like one evangelist who attended that community meeting. While I spoke about what God had shared with me regarding ex-offenders, she looked at me and said, "I'm focusing on at-risk youths!" Her organization was trying to survive. I understood where she was. It had happened to me with the learning center when we were in desperate need for funds. She was so driven to keep herself and her organization alive that fear was driving her from the voice of God. She had become limited by what she feared and what she thought.

God shared with me that it is His wisdom, favor, and guidance that lead us out of problems and into prosperity. His wisdom is what you trust in—not money. He continued, "Money does not solve problems, it only makes men not deal with real issues. My son, do you see why wisdom, My leading, is better than silver and gold? It's your permanent solution to all your needs and dilemmas."

The universal point in these examples is this. When God tells you to do something, how committed are you to doing it, even in the midst of opposition? Are you willing to be on the firing line for God's perfect will for your life? Part of His good work in us is to build us to a point that we can consistently do just that—follow through with His instructions no matter what.

As you hear God daily and do what He tells you to do, trust that He will do His part. That gets Him moving. Your trust in Him opens the way for His part or will to be done.

You will know God's power is working in your life when situations and circumstances, meetings and grant proposals, recommendations and plans are constantly working to His kingdom advantage. You know when His power is working in your life. You know it! And inwardly you know that you don't have to get it done "perfectly" or "say just the right things," because it's not totally dependent upon your ability. *All you need to do is the work of obeying God.* How simple is that?

The Ultimate Example

Jesus had an assignment from God with which none of ours could ever compare. He was chosen from birth to die as a sacrifice for us. He went through excruciating physical abuse accompanied by death on the cross, was made sin, and most painful of all, He was separated from the Father for the first time in all creation. Because He was made sin, he was sent to the lowest pit of hell in our place and was tormented by satan himself and every perverted demon (see Ps. 22:12-13).

Through all this, Jesus willfully obeyed God. He, the last Adam (see 1 Cor. 15:45), did what the first Adam did not. When faced with temptation, which you can be sure will always come in a form that looks good and is desirable, the Lord Jesus Christ said, *"nevertheless, not My will, but Thine, be done"* (Luke 22:42). The temptation for Him was the option to choose His own way, instead of God's perfect way. Rest assured that there were a lot of ways that looked more desirable than the cross. However, the Lord Jesus Christ willfully surrendered His will to the perfect will of His Father. Jesus knew God's perfect will for Him was always to His advantage.

He simply let go of His desires. He buried them and yielded Himself totally without reservation to His Father. In His mind, His desires were dead. It made no difference how hard His flesh pressured Him or how strong His own ambitions might have been. He had no other option because His desires were already dead and buried: *"For Christ did not please Himself [gave no thought to His own interests]…"* (Rom. 15:3 AMP). He completely entrusted Himself and His future to His Father and declared, *"Not My will, but Thine, be done"* (Luke 22:42).

This was a crucial point in Jesus's life, and He passed the test. He declared God's will be done in His life, and this allowed

God to complete man's restoration plan for us, and His ultimate destiny for Jesus, which among other things was to be *"King of Kings, and Lord of Lords"* (Rev. 19:16). This is also the place where Adam blew it. When faced with a similar test with the Tree of the Knowledge of Good and Evil, he chose to follow his own will. And as we know, Adam's decision prohibited God from fulfilling His perfect will for him, which was to *"have dominion...over all the earth"* (Gen. 1:26). Instead of Adam being the ruler, as God designed, he became the ruled and gave his power to a spiritual outlaw, satan. Until Adam gave it to him through disobedience, satan had no legal right to operate in this earth. He, satan, was given power that he had no right to as a spirit being. God had given dominion of the earth to human beings who possessed a physical body so they could rule over this physical world.

Sadly, loss, heartache, and sorrow are the results when we choose to do things our own way instead of God's way. Someone or something else ends up with what was meant for us. Foolishly, we deny God permission to fulfill His destiny in our lives, and we give away the only thing that will ever fulfill us: the opportunity to fulfill God's perfect will on earth.

Let's give God permission to fulfill His perfect will in our lives. Declare aloud every day, *"Father in the mighty name of Jesus Christ, I declare, 'Thy kingdom come and Thy perfect will be done in my life today!'"* (see Matt. 6:10).

Will to Obey and Will to Trust

Make a willful decision. Decide to obey God. Make pleasing Him the first priority in your life daily and throughout the day. Colossians 1:18 says He is to have first place in everything. All God needs is a willing spirit to cooperate with Him. He said, *"If you are willing and obedient, you shall eat the good of the land"* (Isa. 1:19 AMP). *He has provided us with the power to obey. Our part is to provide Him with the will to obey.*

Lack of commitment and trust in God will keep you from His perfect will for you. If you are experiencing an unexplainable lack of provision and direction, perhaps you lack full commitment and trust in God. Perhaps something or someone in your life is inhibiting that trust. Therefore, you continue to settle for the safe, *what-you-know-and-can-reason-with-in-your-own-mind* road, even though deep down you know you are not fully obeying God. Don't be deceived: partial obedience is still disobedience. Disobedience does not yield God's favor and provision.

If this is your situation, set your heart to wholly sell out to God and His perfect will for you. Stop justifying your actions and ask Him to show you what it is that is keeping you from trusting Him fully. It may be a generational issue you have inherited that runs in your family. It may be a wrong that was done to you that you have not forgiven and released from your life. Or it may be that you are just being stubborn and selfish. Whatever it is, God can remove it. God can heal it. Just go to

Him with it! He wants to show you what it is and deal with it once and for all in your life. I urge you to yield to Him completely. He is longing to help you. He does not want you walking around cutting off His power from working in your life any longer. He wants you restored to your original state. He wants you completely dependent upon His ability and His power in you to rule over and control yourself and your circumstances.

Action Point

Let's pray:

Heavenly Father, I want to be fully committed, and I want to trust You completely. Please reveal to me those things in my life that are in any way hindering me. (Pause and let God speak, and then write down what He says to you.)

Now I cast them completely on You, and I ask for Your guidance to show me what steps I must take to separate them from my life forever. (Again, pause and write down what God speaks to you. This will be your action plan.)

Thank You for Your guidance. In the mighty name of Jesus Christ, I commit to do these things immediately. Amen!

Glory to God! I believe there is breakthrough happening right now.

A Willful Decision Study Guide

Study to shew thyself approved unto God, a workman that needeth not to be ashamed, rightly dividing the word of truth.

—2 Timothy 2:15

1. **Joshua 24:15,** *"...as for me and my house, we will serve the Lord."*

2. **God Respects Our Decisions**

    A. Romans 10:9-10, *"...if thou shalt confess with thy mouth the Lord Jesus..."*

    B. Deuteronomy 28:1, *"And it shall come to pass, if thou shalt hearken diligently unto the voice of the Lord thy God..."*

3. **Choosing God's Will Requires Courage (On the Firing Line)**

   A. Joshua 1:9, *"Have not I commanded thee? Be strong and of a good courage..."*

   B. Psalm 27:14, *"...be of good courage, and He shall strengthen thine heart..."*

4. **The Fruit of Obedience**

   A. Deuteronomy 28:1-14, *"...And all these blessings shall come on thee, and overtake thee, if thou shalt hearken unto the voice of the Lord thy God..."*

   B. Genesis 22:18, *"And in thy seed shall all the nations of the earth be blessed; because thou hast obeyed My voice."*

   C. Isaiah 48:18, *"O that thou hadst hearkened to My commandments! Then had thy peace been as a river..."*

   D. Psalm 1:3, *"...and whatsoever he doeth shall prosper."*

   E. Ephesians 6:13-14, *"...Stand therefore, having your loins girt about with truth..."*

5. **Jesus, Our Example**

   A. Luke 22:42, *"...nevertheless not My will, but Thine, be done."*

   B. Romans 15:3, *"For even Christ pleased not Himself..."*

   C. Matthew 4:1-11: The temptation in the wilderness.

D. Jesus excels where Adam failed

a. Genesis 1:26, *"...and let them have dominion..."*

b. Genesis 3:1-24, *"...So He drove out the man."*

c. Matthew 3:17, *"...This is My beloved Son, in whom I am well pleased."*

d. Jude 1:25, *"...be glory and majesty, dominion and power..."*

e. Revelations 19:16, *"...King of Kings and Lord of Lords."*

6. Decide to Obey God (Will to Obey and Will to Trust)

A. Matthew 6:10, *"Thy kingdom come, Thy will be done..."*

B. Colossians 1:18, *"...who is the beginning, the firstborn from the dead; that in all things he might have the preeminence."*

C. Isaiah 1:19, *"If ye be willing and obedient, ye shall eat the good of the land."*

D. Psalm 31:1, *"In Thee, O Lord, do I put my trust..."*

7. Pray for God's Guidance

Notes

Notes

Chapter 4

Matters of the Heart

When we began this study of the paths that lead to living the good life, we started looking from the outside. We began by examining our current state of affairs and accepting that something was out of order. Then we moved inward to examine our relationships. Why do they exist? Are they pure or motivated by a selfish desire or need? Are they positive relationships that would support our pursuit of God's perfect will, or are they hindering ones that would keep us focused on doing things our way rather than God's way?

Our most recent move was even further inward. We now had a decision to make—a willful decision. We had to consider how willing or unwilling we were to stand up for what God wanted done even in the face of opposition. I'm sure many of us had to repent for being cowards in the past and ask God for help to use the power He has given us to overcome the hindrances revealed to us. We took stock of those things and people we needed to separate from and began to execute the action plan God showed us in prayer.

Now we'll go even deeper to the "heart" of the matter because living the good life—committing to live a life totally submitted to God's perfect will—requires a pure heart.

Let's continue.

Jesus, Our Example: How to Walk in God's Perfect Will

Thank God for Jesus! He showed us how to walk in God's perfect will (God's best) for our lives by always being willing to please His Father, regardless of how great the pressure on Him: *"So Jesus said, 'When you lift up the Son of Man, then you will know that I am He, and I do nothing on My own initiative, but I speak these things as the Father taught Me. And He who sent Me is with Me; He has not left Me alone, for* ***I always do the things that are pleasing to Him'"*** (John 8:28-29 NASB).

Jesus's example holds the key to continual victory over our will and disobedient thoughts. Here it is: *become obedient with all your heart!* In other words, with all your heart, be willing to obey God and always do the things that are pleasing to Him.

God asks us to wholly devote our hearts to Him. Radically and without hesitation, He asks us to completely, wholeheartedly give Him our love and devotion daily. Why? Because He is an expert on our individual hearts, and He knows that this is the state that makes our hearts pure (i.e., good soil, see Luke 8:15) and allows Him to produce much fruit in our lives. It's the pure state that He originally created, a state where you are totally fulfilled, or as He puts it in Colossians 2:10, you are "*...made full and having come to fullness of life*" (AMP). This is a state where you are constantly seeking Him and you strongly desire to be with Him; where you delight to keep His Word and fulfill His perfect will for your life; and where you allow Him to lead you by His Spirit and frequently communicate with Him throughout the day. This is a state where you are very determined to walk in permanent obedience to Him. You and He are one; His perfect will is your will, His plans are your plans, His desires are your desires, His thoughts are your thoughts, His ways are your ways, His dreams are your dreams, and His life is your life. This is what it means to truly love your Heavenly Father.

Let's declare daily, *"I am in the Father, and the Father is in me, and we are in perfect harmony!"*

To Love Is to Be Loyal

In relationships, we use phrases like, "I give you my heart" to express our total commitment to another person. In this sense, the heart refers to love and devotion. So what we are really saying is, "I give you my love and devotion." Love can be defined as a deep and tender feeling of affection for, or attachment or devotion to, a person or persons. Devotion means loyalty and deep affection. Devotion comes from the root word *devote*, meaning "to dedicate by vow."[1]

Therefore, when you give God your heart—or devote your heart to Him—you are saying, "I attach myself to You. I will be loyal and faithful to You. I commit to You. I will make vows to You." Anything sound familiar here? Sounds kind of like a marriage covenant, doesn't it? Exactly! This is where the concept of marriage came from. It is a celebration of exchange, where you begin your new partnership with God by completely devoting yourself to Him in all purity, and He completely and totally devotes Himself to you. Revelations 19:7 says: *"Let us rejoice and be glad and give the glory to Him, for the marriage of the Lamb has come and His bride has made herself ready"* (NASB). We are the Bride of the Lord Jesus Christ, and we are making ourselves ready to receive Him by daily giving Him our love and devotion.

Men and women entering marriage express their love and devotion for one another through wedding vows spoken aloud at the marriage ceremony and then support those vows throughout the marriage by remaining loyal to them. *This is exactly how our relationship with God is supposed to be.* Remember, the concept of marriage was designed by God to be the earthly example of our love relationship with Him. He wants us to attach ourselves to Him. He wants us to be loyal and faithful to Him. He wants us to be committed and make vows to

Him. To vow means to promise solemnly, to give, consecrate, or dedicate by a solemn promise.[2] God wants us to make solemn promises to Him, promises that we are dedicated to and serious about performing.

Aren't promises to love, cherish, and care for, until death do we part, made during the marriage ceremony? Likewise, does not God make many wonderful, solemn promises to us? Sure He does! For example, here's just one of His *"precious and magnificent promises"* (2 Pet. 1:4) to us: *"...I will not in any way fail you nor give you up nor leave you without support. [I will] not, [I will] not, [I will] not in any degree leave you helpless nor forsake nor let [you] down (relax My hold on you)! [Assuredly not!]"* (Heb. 13:5 AMP). He is so dedicated and committed to every promise that He wrote them down in His Word and then swore an oath in blood of His Son that He would perform them in our lives (see Heb. 6:17-20). That is truly wonderful!

Are you willing to give God the same kind of devotion that He willingly gives you? How can one have relationship with another if their devotion is not the same? God calls this being *unequally yoked*, and He says not to do it (see 2 Cor. 6:14-15). Do you see the wisdom of God? *God knows that it takes mutual devotion for relationships to work, and this is why He is asking us for it.* He wants a devoted relationship where there is nothing you won't do for Him and there is nothing He won't do for you. Glory to God! That's what a real relationship with Him is all about!

Solemn Promises

God only asks us to make two solemn promises. Jesus made these very clear to us in Mark 12:29-31: *"Jesus answered, 'The foremost is, Hear, O Israel! The Lord our God is one Lord; and you shall love the Lord your God with all your heart, and with all your soul, and with all your mind, and with all your strength. The second is this, You shall love your neighbor as yourself.' There is no other commandment greater than these"* (NASB).

Action Point

Let's do so. Let's express our devotion to Him by making two solemn promises that we are dedicated to and serious to perform.

> *Heavenly Father, I promise to love You with all my heart, all my soul, all my mind, and all my strength, and I promise to love my neighbor as myself. I am dedicated and serious to perform these because I know there is nothing more important to You than these commandments. I promise these to You in the name of Jesus Christ. Amen!*

I encourage you to write down these promises. Your Heavenly Father wrote down every one of His promises to you. Write them down, sign and date them, and then make copies and post them in places where you will see them often. Then every time you see them throughout the day, simply think of Him, and tell your Heavenly Father, *"I love You with all my heart, all my soul, all my mind, and all my strength, and because You desire it, I love my neighbor as myself."*

Endnotes

1. See http://www.yourdictionary.com/devote.

2. Noah Webster, *An American Dictionary of the English Language* (New York, NY: Johnson Reprint Corp., 1970, 1828).

Matters of the Heart Study Guide

Study to shew thyself approved unto God, a workman that needeth not to be ashamed, rightly dividing the word of truth.

—2 Timothy 2:15

1. **Love and Devotion**

   A. Acts 13:22-23, "*...David the son of Jesse, a man after My own heart, who will do all My will...*" (NASB).

2. **Jesus Our Example**

   A. John 8:28-29, "*...I always do the things that are pleasing to Him*" (NASB).

   B. Matthew 22:37, "*...Thou shalt love the Lord thy God with all thy heart...*"

   C. Become obedient with all your heart.

a. Romans 6:17, *"...you became obedient from the heart..."* (NASB).

b. John 14:15, *"If ye love Me, keep My commandments."*

3. The Devoted Heart

A. God desires us to wholly devote our hearts to Him.

a. 2 Corinthians 11:2, *"For I am jealous over you with godly jealousy: for I have espoused you to one husband...as a chaste virgin to Christ."*

b. Exodus 34:14, *"For thou shalt worship no other god: for the Lord, whose name is Jealous, is a jealous God."*

c. Jeremiah 24:7, *"And I will give them an heart to know me, that I am the Lord...for they shall return unto me with their whole heart."*

d. Psalm 73:1, *"Truly God is good to Israel, even to such as are of a clean heart."*

B. Wholehearted devotion purifies the heart, making it good ground for bearing fruit.

a. Psalm 51:10, *"Create in me a clean heart, O God; and renew a right spirit within me."*

b. Luke 8:15 "*...But that on good ground are they, which in an honest and good heart...bring forth fruit...*"

C. The pure heart allows for total life fulfillment.

   a. Colossians 2:10, *"...made full and having come to the fullness of life"* (AMP).

   b. Psalm 24:3-5, *"He that hath clean hands, and a pure heart...He shall receive the blessing from the Lord..."*

   c. Psalm 36:7-8, *"...They shall be abundantly satisfied with the fatness of Thy house; and Thou shalt make them drink of the river of Thy pleasures."*

   d. Psalm 145:19-20, *"He will fulfill the desire of them that fear Him...The Lord preserveth all them that love Him..."*

D. The devoted heart continually seeks after and pursues God.

   a. Matthew 6:33, *"But seek ye first the kingdom of God...and all these things shall be added to you."*

   b. Psalm 119:2, *"Blessed are they that keep His testimonies, and that seek Him with the whole heart."*

   c. Psalm 1:2, *"But his delight is in the law of the Lord; and in His law doth He meditate day and night."*

   d. Psalm 27:4, *"One thing have I desired of the Lord, that will I seek after; that I may dwell in the house of the Lord all the days of my life..."*

e. First Peter 2:2, *"As newborn babes, desire the sincere milk of the word, that ye may grow thereby."*

f. Isaiah 55:6, *"Seek ye the Lord while He may be found, call ye upon Him while He is near."*

E. The devoted heart seeks God's thoughts, plans, and direction.

a. Isaiah 55:7-11, *"...For My thoughts are not your thoughts, neither are your ways My ways, saith the Lord...My ways* [are] *higher than your ways..."*

b. Proverbs 3:6, *"In all thy ways acknowledge Him, and He will direct thy paths."*

c. Proverbs 16:9, *"A man's heart deviseth his way: but the Lord directeth his steps."*

d. Psalm 10:4, *"The wicked, through the pride of his countenance, will not seek after God: God is not in all his thoughts."*

F. Devotion toward God is similar to the devotion of a marriage covenant.

a. Genesis 17: God makes an everlasting covenant with Abraham

b. Psalm 89:34, *"My covenant will I not break, nor alter the thing that is gone out of my lips."*

c. Ephesians 5:24, *"Therefore as the church is subject unto Christ, so let the wives be to their own husbands in every thing."*

d. Ephesians 5:25, *"Husbands, love your wives, even as Christ also loved the church, and gave Himself for it."*

e. Revelations 19:7, *"...give the glory to Him, for the marriage of the Lamb has come and His bride has made herself ready"* (NASB).

G. Daily give God love and devotion. Confess, *"I am in the Father, and the Father is in me, and we are in perfect harmony."*

a. John 10:30, *"I and My Father are one."*

b. John 10:38, *"...believe, that the Father is in Me, and I in Him."*

c. John 17:21, *"...as Thou, Father, art in Me, and I in Thee, that they also may be one in Us..."*

4. **To Love Is to Be Loyal**

A. Define *love.*

B. Define *devotion.*

C. Compare marriage vows and promises to our relationship with God.

a. Marriage was designed by God to be the earthly example of our love relationship with Him.

    i. Jeremiah 3:14, *"Turn, O backsliding children, saith the Lord; for I am married unto you…"*

    ii. Isaiah 54:5, *"…For thy Maker is thine husband; the Lord of hosts is His name…"*

    iii. Isaiah 62:5, *"…as the bridegroom rejoiceth over the bride, so shall thy God rejoice over thee."*

    iv. Revelation 21:2, *"…new Jerusalem, coming down from God out of heaven, prepared as a bride adorned for her husband."*

    v. Revelation 21:9, *"…Come hither, I will shew thee the bride, the Lamb's wife."*

b. Husbands and wives support their marriage vows by remaining loyal to them.

    i. 1 Corinthians 7:33, *"But he that is married careth for…how he may please his wife."*

    ii. 1 Corinthians 7:34, *"…but she that is married careth for…how she may please her husband."*

    iii. Ephesians 5:33, *"Nevertheless let everyone of you in particular so love his wife even as himself; and the wife see that she reverence her husband."*

c. God made and keeps His promises to us.

i. 2 Peter 1:4, *"...precious and magnificent promises..."* (NASB).

ii. Hebrews 13:5, *"...I will not in any degree leave you helpless nor forsake nor let [you] down..."* (AMP).

iii. Hebrews 6:17-20, *"Wherein God...to shew unto the heirs of promise the immutability of His counsel, confirmed it by an oath..."*

d. Be willing to give God the same type of devotion He gives to you.

i. Isaiah 1:19, *"If ye be willing and obedient, ye shall eat the good of the land."*

ii. Amos 3:3, *"Can two walk together, except they be agreed?"*

iii. Mark 12:30, *"...love the Lord thy God with all thy heart..."*

iv. 1 John 4:19, *"We love Him, because He first loved us."*

v. Revelation 2:4, *"...thou hast left thy first love."*

5. Two Solemn Promises to God

A. Mark 12:29-31, *"...love the Lord your God with all your heart...love your neighbor as yourself..."* (NASB).

B. Continually declare before God, *"Heavenly Father, I love You with all my heart, all my soul, all my mind, and all my strength, and because You desire it, I love my neighbor as myself."*

C. Love for God fuels everything in the Kingdom of God.

   a. Galatians 5:6, *"...faith which worketh by love..."*

   b. Hebrews 6:10, *"For God is not unrighteous to forget your work and labour of love, which ye have shown toward His name..."*

D. Love for God must be the motivation behind everything you do, and desire.

   a. Matthew 6:33, *"...seek ye first the kingdom of God, and His righteousness..."*

   b. John 14:15, *"If ye love Me, keep My commandments."*

   c. Romans 13:8, *"Owe no man any thing, but to love one another: for he that loveth another hath fulfilled the law."*

   d. 2 Corinthians 8:24, *"Wherefore shew ye to them...the proof of your love..."*

Notes

Notes

Chapter 5

Purify Your Heart

THERE IS NOTHING MORE IMPORTANT than your love relationship with your Heavenly Father. It's what makes everything in the Kingdom of God work. Listen carefully: Faith works through love (see Gal. 5:6). Everything you do, everything you believe God for right now, must have love for God as its motive. Sure, you want to get your bills paid and live a prosperous life. God wants this for you too (see 3 John 2). But you must set your heart on God and the advancement of His Kingdom on earth first. Remember, Jesus said, *"But seek first His Kingdom and His righteousness; and all these things will be added to you"* (Matt. 6:33 NASB).

Simply obey God's instructions in James 4:8: *"...purify your hearts, you double minded"* (NASB). Being double minded is having two motives. Your faith will not work this way because your heart will be divided in devotion and thus impure toward God. You must make a choice. Don't try to fool God like Saul (see 1 Sam. 15). He knows your heart, so don't ever try to deceive Him in any way. He doesn't like it!

No Man Can Serve Two Masters

Have you ever thought, *"I'm doing everything I know to do. I'm tithing, and I'm giving. I'm praying this special prayer, giving in this special offering, and serving with my time and talents, but it's just not producing for me. The windows of Heaven seem to be shut up over my life, and that's not scriptural. What am I doing wrong? Am I doing anything right?"*

If you have, I totally understand where you're coming from. I can't say I ever got mad at preachers and their prosperity messages because I knew it was God's will for me to prosper (see John 10:10). But I could probably say that I was jealous or maybe, more truthfully, frustrated by them. I was tithing and giving, but nothing was happening for me. Disgusted, I'd look at them and think, *"Man this ain't working for me; it's working for him, but it ain't happening for me. Sure, look at what he's got. Of course it's working for him. He's got a large congregation, a television following, books and tapes all over the world—of course he's living in abundance."* I got focused on the external of what these preachers had in abundance rather than the internal abundance that produced the external.

I had to realize that there were things in my life that were blocking my blessings. Something was wrong. My tithes wouldn't fix it. My offerings wouldn't fix it. Going to church wouldn't fix it. My good works wouldn't fix it. There were deeper things that had to be corrected to allow God's blessing to flow in my life.

What would fix it? What were the deeper things?

1. I Lacked a Pure Heart.

I had an impure heart. My motives and purposes were based in fear and selfishness.

My prayers became pleadings and convincing sessions to God for why He should bless me, because I did tithe. True, I was tithing, but there was no power there. I was not increasing. If you are giving or tithing and not increasing, then something is wrong! Malachi 3:10 says, *"Bring ye all the tithes into the storehouse, that there may be meat in Mine house, and prove Me now herewith, saith the Lord of hosts, if I will not open you the windows of heaven, and pour you out a blessing, that there shall not be room enough to receive it."* My heart was contaminated. The ground from which my pseudo-obedience came couldn't produce the promised fruit of the open windows of Heaven.

There are people who grew up in the church and have been saved for a while who find themselves in a similar situation. They say in their hearts, just as I did, *"I did all that; it's not working. Now what?"* They can easily get caught up seeking out the next sure-fire method or formula. Many become shipwrecked in their faith and turn to handling their business and personal affairs the world's way. Then they get into condemnation, which leads them down a bad path.

2. I Was Doing Things out of Fear and Tradition.

I was tithing and giving like I was playing the lottery; if I just did enough of it, then I was bound to hit the jackpot one day. I dreamed my phone would ring, or an envelope would come in the mail, and my days of suffering would be over. This was foolishness because my giving and tithing was not based on my love for God and trusting Him to honor His Word but rather what I could get out of it.

The lesson: Hear and do based upon what God directs. Do because of love and obedience—period. Do not do because of fear that the need is not going to be met or because of guilty feelings. Obey God's Word, and do what God tells you to do simply because you love Him and want to please Him. We need to stop doing things to justify ourselves to God. Jesus Christ is our righteousness—not any of our good works! Believe that and do things because you love Him.

3. I Was Sabotaging God's Blessing on My Life.

As you might recall, I thought I was doing the right thing by helping with the learning center. On the contrary, my involvement with the business and dealing with the issues that surrounded keeping it afloat were actually keeping me from my destiny in God's perfect will.

After shutting down the operation, I thought about what stopped me from doing the good work I envisioned for the learning center, and here's what I learned.

We all have a certain "lane" or field of work or ministry where we are going to do our best. Other opportunities come along, even closely related opportunities, that we *can* do, but they are not God's perfect will for us. These other opportunities tend to appeal to us, because we can do them or because they come with some other promise of fulfilling a certain desire or dream we have. So, rather than obtaining permission from our Commander-in-Chief, the Lord Jesus Christ, regarding our involvement, we stubbornly move forward because it's really something *we want to do.*

The learning center was a "good thing." It just wasn't *my* thing or Flying HIGH's thing. Did I learn from it? Absolutely! I learned from it and made life changes otherwise it would have destroyed me. The apostle Paul wrote in Philippians 2:12-13, *"...work out your salvation with fear and trembling; for it is God who is at work in you, both to will and to work His good pleasure"* (NASB). I believe he said this because he knew all of us would have to work our way into God's perfect will. He knew this would only happen if we were yielded to God's leading and command every day—literally, that we are afraid to do anything that is outside of His perfect will for our lives. Therefore, we are always allowing Him to have His way in our lives and working with Him in all our endeavors and relationships.

It's because of our own selfishness, stubbornness, and disobedience that we get into sabotaging ourselves. I thought the learning center was an opportunity for me to use my skills and experience to do good, but it wasn't the place for me to do the most good; it was outside of God's perfect will for me. Yet I trusted more in my ability to sustain my family in the business than in God's ability. I was determined to make it work, even as I saw the handwriting on the wall plainly spelling out F-A-I-L-I-N-G.

The lesson: Three things keep us back from doing our *best* good:

1. Selfishness
2. Stubbornness
3. Disobedience

These three were keeping me from walking in God's perfect will, sabotaging me, and delaying me from getting to my destiny. The blessings He had for me were not coming because I was not on the perfect path.

If my story sounds like yours, believe it or not, you're more fear-driven than you are faith-driven. You hear one guy say, "Do this"—so you do it. You hear that guy say, "Do that," so you do it too. You feel like you're grasping for straws, seeking for that breakthrough solution to the lack in your life.

Take a deep breath and exhale slowly. You must examine whether you are doing things for the money or for your love for God. Are you doing the sacrificial giving, praying, and serving because you need the money and you need it to survive, not because you love God? I didn't say you did not love God. I know you do. However, could it be that your motive for tithing, giving, praying, fasting, and serving is coming out of *need* rather than from love?

It's All About You and God

This whole thing, your existence on this earth, is about you and the Lord. It's about you and your relationship with the Lord (how you relate to Him). He really has tunnel vision; He's really not so much concerned about all the stuff that goes on in your life. He is all about you, [your name goes here]. That's what He is all about. He can fix the drama in a heartbeat—once you and He get it together. I will never forget when He said that to me—"It's all about you and Me." I had a hard time understanding it, because I just couldn't believe it's all about Him and me. My self-esteem was too low to receive it. But when all is said and done, it will be you and Him standing there together, and it will all be about you and Him.

You! Your whole life is about you and the Lord—right now, in this time, and in this earth realm. God got me to understand this by showing me my motives for doing things. He did this by using my motives of giving. I was tithing consistently 10 percent of my income. He revealed to me that even though I was doing a good thing by giving, I was using that as my way to make myself "good" rather than giving because He desired it. Basically, I was giving more out of fear than because I loved Him.

As previously mentioned, I was around sports most of my life and made myself very performance-driven. If I played well, I was good. If I didn't, I was bad. This happens often with athletes and others whose performance is out front. I got caught up identifying my performance with my identity. When I transitioned to life off the field, I still kept this attitude that I had to make myself a good person by my performance. However, God was teaching me that I was a good person because of our relationship; that's what makes me a good person. It's because we are in harmony and moving together, not because I am doing things that are performance-driven.

Money-Motivated Performance: Fire Fear and Hire Faith

Seven people interviewed for a position within our organization. One person followed up with a call and a letter. The person was not really suited for the position, but I thought it was an honorable thing that she did, so I had her come back in to see if there was something that maybe we missed during the interviews. After speaking with her for a while, she confessed, "I really need the money." She had followed the rules of interview etiquette, not because she really wanted to be considered for the job, but because she really needed money—two different motives for achieving the same outcome. Needless to say, our conversation turned to, "How can we help?" rather than, "When can you start?"

Faith says Jesus has already paid the price to get me the money. I have authority over the provision because of what Jesus did for me. Therefore, I command that provision to come forth. I declare that God will direct my path (of thinking) and order my steps (of doing), and lead me in the way that I should go. He will supply all of my needs according to His riches in glory (see Phil. 4:19).

When you get the revelation that Jesus became poor so that you can be rich and that you are seated again with Him in heavenly places (your mind thinks on a higher level), you realize that money is just another thing that you have dominion over, and it really does have to listen to you.

Depend on His ability to bring it to you and not your own. When you make a demand on provision, in faith, God will do His part and get it to you.

Purify Your Motives; Purify Your Heart!

You can purify your heart by purifying your motives. Rather than desiring to get your bills paid, sincerely desire to honor the blood of Jesus (or Jesus' death on the cross) and glorify the work He has done to provide you with financial abundance, which will position you with the ability to get your bills paid. Change your desire to possess wealth into one to establish the Kingdom of God upon the earth and have more than enough for every good deed, so that you might help others.

God is very straightforward in His instructions to us. *"**Whatever you do,** do your work heartily, **as for the Lord rather than for men,** knowing that **from the Lord you will receive the reward** of the inheritance. It is the Lord Christ whom you serve"* (Col. 3:23-24 NASB). Every single thing you are believing God for in your life, do out of your love for Him. If you cannot do it to honor Him, then you have no business being involved in it. I believe this is where most of us are missing it and why we are so frustrated and feel God is not coming through for us. Our minds have been so clouded with selfishness that we have left our first love (see Rev. 2:4) in pursuit of our own agendas.

Even in the midst of pursuing "good" things that we know God has called us to do, we think it's all about us, our vision, and what we can achieve for God. We become enamored with trying to impress others and esteeming ourselves. We do this instead of simply allowing God to use us as His vessels of honor to do His work, His way, so that He is able to receive all the glory and draw men to His goodness. Come on; let's wake up to this truth! *You must allow God to do His work, His way, through you and then allow Him to receive all the glory for it; this is the ultimate expression of your love for Him!* Freely give Him your total obedience, and freely give Him all the glory for all the good He does through you! Freely do so with no strings attached and no hidden agendas. Isn't this exactly the way Jesus lived His life? Isn't it also why God exalted Him and gave Him a name above every name in heaven, on earth, and under the earth (see Phil. 2:5-11)? Absolutely!

I like this message I found written on one of those daily calendars; it will help keep God's will for your life in the right perspective.

> I believe with all my heart that it is impossible to be both goal-oriented and God-oriented at the same time. One orientation will always take precedence over the other. When our desires to achieve take the lead, several things happen in our relationship with God. He becomes a means to an end rather than the end. We tend to use God rather than worship Him. We find ourselves seeking information about Him rather than transformation by Him.[1]

Ask God to strengthen you daily so He can carry out His perfect will for your life.

Action Point

A great prayer is located in Hebrews 13:21 (AMP). Let's pray:

> *Father, in the mighty name of Jesus Christ, I ask that You strengthen (complete, perfect) and make me what I ought to be and equip me with everything good that You may carry out Your will; (while You Yourself) work in me and accomplish that which is pleasing in Your sight, through Jesus Christ (the Messiah); to whom be the glory forever and ever (to the ages of the ages). Amen (so be it).*

Endnote

1. Charles Stanley, *A Touch of His Freedom* (Grand Rapids, MI: Zondervan Publishing, 1991).

Purify Your Heart Study Guide

Study to shew thyself approved unto God, a workman that needeth not to be ashamed, rightly dividing the word of truth.

—2 Timothy 2:15

1. **Purify Your Heart**

   A. To be double minded is to have two motives, causing a divided and impure heart toward God, which keeps faith from working.

      a. James 4:8, "*...purify your hearts, ye double minded.*"

      b. Isaiah 55:7, "*Let the wicked forsake his way, and the unrighteous man his thoughts...*"

   B. Matthew 6:24, "*No man can serve two masters...*"

C. Revelation 2:4, *"...you have left your first love..."* (NASB).

D. Joshua 24:15, *"...choose you this day whom ye will serve...but as for me and my house, we will serve the Lord."*

2. No Man Can Serve Two Masters

A. Impure heart: motives based in fear and selfishness

a. Philippians 2:3, *"Let nothing be done through strife or vainglory..."*

b. Galatians 5:20-21, *"...selfish ambition, dissension, division...anyone living that sort of life will not inherit the Kingdom of God"* (NLT).

c. Shipwrecked faith

i. 1 Timothy 1:19, *"keeping faith and a good conscience, which some have rejected and suffered shipwreck in regard to their faith"* (NASB).

ii. Matthew 8:26, *"And He saith unto them, 'Why are ye fearful, O ye of little faith?'"*

B. Performance-driven: fear and tradition

a. Mark 7:8, *"...laying aside the commandment of God, ye hold the tradition of men..."*

b. Mark 7:13, *"Making the word of God of none effect through your tradition..."*

c. Matthew 6:2, "...*do not sound a trumpet before thee, as the hypocrites do in the synagogues and in the streets, that they may have glory of men."*

d. Hear and do based on God's direction.

   i. Proverbs 3:6, *"In all thy ways acknowledge Him, and He shall direct thy paths."*

   ii. John 2:5, "...*Whatsoever He saith unto you, do it."*

   iii. Luke 8:21, "...*My mother and my brethren are these which hear the word of God, and do it."*

e. Jesus Christ is our righteousness.

   i. Jeremiah 23:6, "...*whereby He shall be called, The Lord Our Righteousness."*

   ii. Romans 5:17, "...*the gift of righteousness shall reign in life by one, Jesus Christ."*

C. Beware of self-sabotage

a. Proverbs 10:14, "...*but the mouth of the foolish is near destruction."*

b. Proverbs 14:14, *"The backslider in heart shall be filled with his own ways..."*

c. Isaiah 55:7, *"Let the wicked forsake his way, and the unrighteous man his thoughts..."*

d. Philippians 3:19, *"Whose end is destruction, whose God is their belly, and whose glory is in their shame, who mind earthly things."*

e. Hindrances to walking in God's perfect will:

   i. Selfishness: Jude 16, *"...walking after their own lusts...having men's persons in admiration because of advantage."*

   ii. Stubbornness: Judges 2:19-23, *"...they ceased not from their own doings, nor from their stubborn way...Therefore the Lord left those nations..."*

   iii. Disobedience: Deuteronomy 11:28, *"And a curse, if ye will not obey the commandments of the Lord your God..."*

f. Fear-driven vs. faith-driven

   i. James 1:8, *"A double minded man is unstable in all his ways."*

   ii. Job 3:25, *"For the thing which I greatly feared is come upon me..."*

   iii. Psalm 34:4, *"...and delivered me from all my fears."*

iv. Mark 4:40, *"...Why are ye so fearful? How is it that ye have no faith?"*

v. 2 Corinthians 7:5, *"...without were fightings, within were fears."*

vi. Galatians 2:20, *"...the life which I now live in the flesh I live by the faith of the Son of God, who loved me..."*

vii. 2 Corinthians 5:7, *"For we walk by faith, not by sight."*

viii. Hebrews 11:1, *"Now faith is the substance of things hoped for, the evidence of things not seen."*

ix. Hebrews 10:38, *"Now the just shall live by faith..."*

x. James 1:6, *"But let him ask in faith, nothing wavering..."*

g. Need for money vs. love for God

i. Fear attitude:

(a) 2 Timothy 1:7, *"For God has not given us a spirit of fear..."*(NASB).

(b) Numbers 13:33, *"And there we saw the giants...and we were in our own sight as grasshoppers..."*

(c) 1 Thessalonians 3:10, "*...might perfect that which is lacking in your faith.*"

ii. Faith attitude

(a) Philippians 4:19, "*God will supply all your needs according to His riches in glory in Christ Jesus*" (NASB).

(b) Romans 8:31, "*...If God be for us, who can be against us?*"

(c) 1 Samuel 17:36, "*Thy servant slew both lion and the bear: and this uncircumcised Philistine shall be as one of them...*"

(d) Romans 4:19-20, "*And being not weak in faith, he considered not his own body now dead...He staggered not at the promise of God through unbelief...*"

D. Be willing to change.

a. Do what God wants *you* to do.

i. Isaiah 1:19-20, "*If ye are willing and obedient, ye shall eat the good of the land; but if ye refuse and rebel, ye shall be devoured with the sword: for the mouth of the Lord hath spoken it.*"

3. It's All About You and God

A. John 17:26, "*...that the love wherewith Thou hast loved Me may be in them, and I in them.*"

B. Psalm 8:4, *"What is man, that Thou art mindful of him..."*

C. Psalm 111:5, *"...He will ever be mindful of His covenant."*

D. Psalm 115:12, *"The Lord hath been mindful of us..."*

E. Psalm 31:14-15, *"...I said, Thou art my God. My times are in Thy hand..."*

F. Psalm 139:1-24, *"How precious also are Thy thoughts unto me, O God! how great is the sum of them!..."*

G. Jeremiah 1:5, *"Before I formed thee in the belly I knew thee..."*

H. Jeremiah 29:11, *"For I know the thoughts that I* [the Lord] *think toward you...thoughts of peace, and not of evil..."*

I. Luke 12:7, *"But even the very hairs of your head are all numbered..."*

J. Isaiah 26:3, *"Thou wilt keep him in perfect peace, whose mind is stayed on Thee..."*

K. John 10:10, *"...I am come that they might have...it* [life] *more abundantly."*

L. John 3:16, *"For God so loved the world, that He gave his only begotten Son, that whosoever believeth in Him should not perish, but have everlasting life."*

M. Self-esteem hinges on your love relationship with God—how you relate to God.

a. Jeremiah 1:8, *"Be not afraid of their faces: for I am with thee to deliver thee…"*

b. Psalm 139:14, *"I will praise Thee; for I am fearfully and wonderfully made…"*

c. Romans 5:8, *"But God commendeth His love toward us, in that, while we were yet sinners, Christ died for us."*

d. 1 John 3:21, *"…if our heart condemn us not, then have we confidence toward God."*

e. Philippians 1:6, *"Being confident of this very thing, that He which hath begun a good work in you will perform it until the day of Jesus Christ."*

f. Matthew 6:26, *"Behold the fowls of the air…Are ye not much better than they?"*

g. 2 Corinthians 6:18, *"And will be a Father unto you, and ye shall be My sons and daughters…"*

h. Romans 8:15, *"…ye have received the Spirit of adoption, whereby we cry, Abba, Father."*

i. Romans 8:16, *"…that we are the children of God."*

4. **Money-Motivated Performance: Performing to Receive Love vs. Receiving Unconditional Love**

   A. Matthew 6:7, *"...for they think that they shall be heard for their much speaking."*

   B. 2 Corinthians 5:21, *"...that we might be made the righteousness of God in Him."*

   C. Romans 4:6, *"...unto whom God imputeth righteousness without works."*

   D. Ephesians 2:8-9, *"For by grace are ye saved through faith...Not of works, lest any man should boast."*

   E. 2 Timothy 1:9, *"...not according to our works, but according to His own purpose and grace..."*

   F. Psalm 6:9, *"...the Lord will receive my prayer."*

   G. To secure success, fire fear and hire faith.

      a. Job 40:7, *"...and declare Thou unto me."*

      b. 2 Corinthians 8:9, *"...that ye through His* [Christ's] *poverty might be rich."*

      c. John 10:10, *"...I am come that they might have life...more abundantly."*

      d. Ephesians 3:20, *"Now unto Him that is able to do exceeding abundantly above all that we can ask or think..."*

e. 3 John 2, "*...I wish above all things that thou mayest prosper and be in health...*"

5. **Purify Motives; Purify Your Heart**

A. 1 Kings 9:4, "*And if thou wilt walk before Me...in integrity of heart...*"

B. Psalm 15:2, "*...and speaketh the truth in his heart.*"

C. Habakkuk 2:4, "*Behold, his soul which is lifted up is not upright in him...*"

D. Philippians 4:8, "*...whatsoever things are pure...think on these things.*"

E. 1 Timothy 1:5, "*...out of a pure heart, and of a good conscience...*"

F. Matthew 6:24, "*No man can serve two masters...*"

G. Matthew 6:33, "*But seek ye first the kingdom of God, and His righteousness...*"

H. Colossians 3:23-26, "*...And whatsoever ye do, do it heartily; as to the Lord, and not unto men...*"

I. Be vessels of honor used by God.

a. Acts 9:15, "*...for he is a chosen vessel unto Me...*"

b. 2 Timothy 2:21, "*If a man therefore purge himself from these, he shall be a vessel unto honour...meet for the master's use...*"

c. 1 Corinthians 6:20, *"For ye are bought with a price: therefore glorify God in your body, and in your spirit, which are God's."*

d. Jesus, our example: Hebrews 12:2, *"Looking unto Jesus…who for the joy that was set before Him endured the cross…"*

J. God gives promotion.

a. Psalm 75:6-7, *"…But God is the judge: He putteth down one, and setteth up another."*

b. 1 Peter 5:6, *"…that He may exalt you in due time…"*

c. Matthew 23:12, *"…and he that humble himself shall be exalted."*

d. Jesus our example: Philippians 2:5-11, *"…Wherefore God also hath highly exalted Him, and given Him a name which is above every name…"*

Notes

Notes

Chapter 6

Selfishness: The Great Manifestation Blocker

LET'S EXPLORE THIS CHARACTER FLAW called *selfishness*. Selfishness stops us from possessing all God has freely given to us and from walking in His perfect will. I believe, more than anything else, selfishness stops the Body of Christ from possessing all that belongs to them. I call it "the great manifestation blocker." There are literally hundreds of examples in the Bible of those who foolishly allowed selfishness to keep them from possessing all God desired to freely give. From Adam to Esau to Judas Iscariot to Ananias and Sapphira, they all robbed themselves of God's blessings and reaped a fateful harvest from their selfish acts.

To consistently walk in permanent obedience and overcome selfishness, we must understand what selfishness is and why we struggle with it. We know from what we read in the Book of James that selfishness is the devil's nature. James 3:14-16: *"But if you are selfish and have bitter jealousy in your hearts, do not brag. Your bragging is a lie that hides the truth. That kind of 'wisdom' does not come from God but from the world. It is not spiritual; it is from the devil. Where jealousy and selfishness are, there will be confusion and every kind of evil"* (NCV).

In Isaiah 14:13-14, God gives us further insight: "*But you said in your heart, I will...I will...and I will...I will...I will...*" (paraphrased). Five times satan says in his heart, "*I will.*" These two words are very powerful. They indicate a decision of the heart. They indicate that the heart will pursue a particular direction, and they express the desire of the heart. In other words, satan thinks of only himself, or "I"; then he makes a decision, or "wills," to pursue his own self-interest. He habitually thinks and acts this way. *He only thinks of himself and only pursues his own self-interest.* It is this kind of thinking that makes him the thief, killer, and destroyer that Jesus said he was in John 10:10. This is also an accurate description of our former sinful nature and its fleshly, selfish thinking.

Remember the attitude I had about the learning center? Do you recall how many "I" thoughts I pursued? *I* put the learning center under Flying HIGH, because *I* was going to make sure it was a viable business, and when it started to go under *I* was not going to let it fail come hell or high water, and *I* was afraid my family would not survive if *I* did not help them, and *I* started seeking relationships based on what people could do for the operation financially...*I, I, I...I* thought only of preserving myself, through my abilities, and *I* pursued my self-interest. In essence, I exalted myself over God. And what happened? My little selfish empire came falling down!

Selfishness Is a Way of Thinking

Selfish ways of thinking are referred to as "the flesh" throughout the Bible. Understand that although we are born again with a new nature in God's likeness, we are still subject to have selfish ways of thinking that God wants us to overcome with His power to resist and separate. This takes hard work because our former sinful nature trained us to think after what *it* wanted. Think about it for a moment. Before you gave your life to Christ, you naturally thought of yourself and naturally pursued your own self-interests. No one had to tell you to do this. It came naturally to you. Think of a child who is always saying, "mine," or always trying to get his own way. This is the behavior ruled by fleshly, selfish thinking from the former sinful nature. Romans 8:5-8 explains this clearly: *Those who are dominated by the sinful nature think about sinful things, but those who are controlled by the Holy Spirit think about things that please the Spirit. So letting your sinful nature control your mind leads to death. But letting the Spirit control your mind leads to life and peace. For the sinful nature is always hostile to God. It never did obey God's laws, and it never will. That's why those who are still under the control of their sinful nature can never please God* (NLT).

Those who are ruled by their flesh, or selfish ways of thinking, cannot please God because they are focused on self-preservation, self-gratification, and self-exaltation, or as First

John 2:16 says, "*the lust of the flesh and the lust of the eyes and the boastful pride of life*" (NASB). They only think of themselves, and they only want to pursue things that are self-pleasing. *In other words, they are habitually driven by a lust or a strong, personal desire to constantly satisfy themselves.*

So we see that selfishness is a way of thinking that came from our former sinful nature. Self thinks only of itself and its own interests or pleasures. *Therefore, I define selfishness as having* ***too much concern for your own welfare and interests and having little or no concern for God and others.*** Selfishness is a form of idolatry. It's self-worship. It's making yourself the focus of your life and thereby making yourself your own god. No wonder God's first commandment is, "*You shall have no other gods before Me*" (Exod. 20:3 NASB). He knew that your flesh would constantly be trying to exalt itself in your life. The flesh, through selfish thinking, says, "Please me, not God. Listen to your sensual urges and desires and pursue them. Do whatever you feel like doing and pay no attention to what God commands and instructs you."

Take it to God

In my learning center experience, I didn't ask for God's direction, so I didn't even have His guidance to pay attention to. I was the god of those decisions and that situation. I didn't realize that my being out of God's perfect will was also impacting my family members. Perhaps if they had pursued the learning center without my involvement, it might still be around today.

What's your story? Take the selfishness examination that follows to find out if you have practiced selfishness by doing any of the following. Find out where you are, and then take the necessary steps to get out of selfishness.

Selfishness Examination

Behavior or Attitude	Yes / No
I refused to forgive.	_____
I slept on the job.	_____
I was ungrateful.	_____
I put my own desires first before others because I feared there wouldn't be enough for me.	_____
I hated people because of their skin color.	_____
I hated people because of their culture.	_____
I was rebellious, stubborn, and unreasonable.	_____
I lived for the moment and took no thought for how my actions would impact others or the future.	_____
I thought making money was my first priority.	_____
I thought life was all about me; me becoming rich, me getting married, me having a family, me having a good job, me being famous and achieving great things.	_____
I slandered, maligned, and talked about others.	_____
I thought violence, immorality, and evil were entertaining.	_____
I thought getting drunk or high was my right.	_____
I was brutal, reckless, angry, and violent.	_____
I thought that my body was my own and I could do whatever I wanted with it: have sex with whomever, kill an unborn baby, do drugs, etc.	_____
I rebelled against God or anybody else who tried to instruct me for my own good.	_____

Behavior or Attitude	**Yes / No**
I was conceited and expected others to do for me.	_____
I hated what was good and loved what was evil.	_____
I enjoyed destroying others and causing them pain.	_____
I caused dissentions and fights.	_____
I loved money and greedily did wrong to get it.	_____
I was arrogant and demanding.	_____
I did right things with wrong motives.	_____
I helped myself to another person's property.	_____
I murdered someone (physically, emotionally, or socially).	_____
I thought that my only real obligation was to myself, regardless of who got hurt.	_____
I thought that my priority in life was to make things easy and pleasant for myself.	_____
I used others for my own gratification through immorality, fornication, adultery, or perversion.	_____
I lied.	_____
I did whatever it took to protect and gratify myself.	_____
I deceived and stole.	_____
I was jealous, envious, and full of strife.	_____
I made excuses and justified myself no matter what I did wrong.	_____

Did any of these resemble thoughts you've had or behavior you've done in any way? Are there others not listed? Take time to jot them down. Highlight those you've dealt with or are dealing with for quick reference during your prayer time. Expose them before God; give them to Him. It won't be long before your attitude and behavior toward those things begin to change.

Get Tough!

We have to get tough with disciplining our thoughts. Like a child needs constant discipline, so we must constantly discipline away our selfish way of thinking until our thoughts come into agreement with God's nature of love within us. We must use the power God restored to us through Jesus, and take authority over fear and selfishness and command them to go from our lives! Then we must make a decision to train ourselves to pursue love—the decision to do for the good of others as directed by God. We must make the decision to think of others, pursue the welfare of others, and act for the advantage of others until it becomes our natural desire. We train ourselves by meditating on First Corinthians 13 and Luke 6:22-23 and 27-38. Through meditation, the presence of God's love found in His Word will flush out any remaining fear. God's Word is always the solution to overcoming fear and selfishness. It has a washing effect upon our thinking (see Eph. 5:26).

If you continue to struggle with fear and selfishness, then you need to get more Word in you through meditation. Remember this: more word = no fear. No word = more fear. Allow God's Word to get deeply rooted in you, so rooted that when you are confronted with a temptation to act selfishly, His Word of love will speak to you from inside. *This is how you know that you have really taken hold of God's Word in your heart: the Word speaks to you in real-life situations.* Then you will know Acts 19:20 has come to manifestation in your life: *"So in a powerful way the word of the Lord kept spreading and growing"* (NCV). Now shout this aloud: *"I will think of others, and I will pursue their interests and do things for their advantage!"*

The pathway to God's blessing is walking in permanent obedience to God in His perfect will. Jesus said this in plain and simple language: *"Enter through the narrow gate. The gate is wide and the road is wide that leads to hell, and many people enter through that gate. But the gate is small and the road is narrow that leads to true life. Only a few people find that road"* (Matt. 7:13-14 NCV). *Be one of the few!* Don't allow yourself or the devil to block you from fulfilling God's perfect will on this earth.

Fear + Selfishness = Struggle

You may ask, "If I have God's nature of love now, why do I still struggle with selfishness?" It's very simple. *We continue to struggle with selfishness because we continue to allow fear to torment and provoke us to return to how we used to think and operate through our old nature.* We fear there won't be enough. We fear God's Word won't come to pass. We fear things won't work out. We fear what other people think of us. We fear we won't be able to overcome the situation, so we go into self-preservation, self-gratification, and self-exaltation mode. Fear is a spiritual force that is constantly trying to pressure us to take things into our own hands and return to our old nature's way of doing things. *Fear is the primary pressure satan uses to try to keep us selfish and only concerned about ourselves.*

Never forget this: satan wants you operating in fear; he wants you concerned only about yourself so you will be unable to receive from God and be a blessing to others, which is God's ultimate purpose for you while on this earth. Did you catch that? *Selfishness is the blocker satan or you can use to stop the manifestation of God's promises and His perfect will in your life.*

Overcoming the Struggle

"Living the good life" requires us to discipline our minds to follow after God regardless of circumstances and situations, emotions, and popular opinions. We can "overcome" daily. Listen to these powerful words in First John 5:5 (NASB): *"Who is the one who overcomes the world, but he who believes that Jesus is the Son of God?"*

The struggle to achieve the life that God has predestined for us is a result of not fully committing ourselves to God's leading. If we trust in the god of ourselves, our thoughts, our education, and our experiences, over what God knows and understands and desires, we will find ourselves struggling to survive, struggling to make ends meet, struggling in relationships, and struggling in our business or ministry endeavors.

To live in God's perfect will we must discipline ourselves to overcome adversity continuously. *If we didn't live in this world, if we didn't live in the flesh and there was no devil, there would be no need to consistently discipline ourselves.*

I've often heard experienced leaders say when teaching about excelling in life, whether personal or professional, ministry or business, "New level, new devil." They mean that adversity doesn't stop coming. The mere fact that we are still in our human bodies leaves us subject to distractions and temptations that would lead us to think and act contrary to how God thinks and acts.

Jesus is our example. He lived "the good life" before us. He continually overcame negative situations. Recall His 40 days in the wilderness. Humanly impacted by the lack of food, water, and basic needs, He still chose to think and make decisions based on what God said over what the devil was saying to Him (see Matt. 4:1-11). How about the ultimate situation in the Garden of Gethsemane? Here Jesus directly asked God if the crucifixion could be taken away from Him. Yet, disciplined in overcoming His human emotions, He declared, *"Nevertheless, not what I will [not what I desire], but as You will and desire"* (Matt. 26:39 AMP).

The Needy Greedy

I suggest that many in the Body of Christ must overcome a "needy" mentality—the "give-it-to-me-for-nothing, hook-me-up handout because I'm a good person doing a good thing" mentality. God promised us favor—not handouts. We must be willing to work and follow God's leadings. We must focus on the instructions God gives us to bring us to victory instead of focusing on the struggle. Heed God's instructions in First Corinthians 15:57-58: *"But thanks be to God, who give us the victory through our Lord Jesus Christ. Therefore, my beloved brethren, be steadfast, immovable, always abounding in the work of the Lord, knowing that your toil is not in vain in the Lord"* (NASB).

Bottom line: not every time we overcome do we have to struggle, but every time we struggle, we can overcome. Overcome whatever is holding you back from totally trusting in God's ability to lead and direct your life. Put His ability to work for you right now. Do it by simply thanking Him for the victory over whatever you are currently dealing with at this time and then keep thanking Him for it! *"You are from God, little children, and have overcome them: because greater is He who is in you than he who is in the world"* (1 John 4:4 NASB).

Selfishness Produces Lack

Another reason selfishness is dangerous is because it opens the door for all sorts of lack to manifest in our lives. Here's what I believe the Lord Jesus Christ spoke to me about this. He said,

> *My people lack because they have their hearts only on themselves. I did not make man to be this way. Man was made to work with Me to subdue the earth by making it into a place where others could dwell in peace, with Me and with one another. This was My intent for man. Man was to continually be seeking the welfare of others so all the principles I established in Heaven would be working in the earth. But when a man only seeks his own, he seeks only to establish himself in the earth and becomes a partner with the devil.*
>
> *The devil's nature is to do what's best for himself regardless of who it hurts. This is why the devil seeks to steal, kill, and destroy—in fear that others will get more than he does. This explains why he fights My Body so fervently. He sees the Body of Christ has access to all he once had and more. That's why he and all who have selfish natures like him will oppose any advancement of My people in the earth.*
>
> *This is also why there were enemies in the Promised Land who fought against My people. They did not want My people to take what I had freely given them. They were*

selfish tools of the devil to stop My people. They were completely under the devil's control. That's why their seed had to be eliminated from the earth—because it would always oppose My people obtaining what is rightfully theirs. Their seed is some of the same people who are still in the earth who will kill all who proclaim My Name.

Now I ask, "Do you want to be a partner with the devil? Do you want to stop yourself or others in the Body of Christ from obtaining all that is rightfully theirs and advancing God's Kingdom on earth?" I didn't think so. Therefore, do not allow selfishness to have any authority in your life! Listen again to James 3:14-16: *"But if you are selfish and have bitter jealousy in your hearts, do not brag. Your bragging is a lie that hides the truth. That kind of 'wisdom' does not come from God but from the world. It is not spiritual; it is from the devil. Where jealousy and selfishness are, there will be confusion and every kind of evil"* (NCV).

Selfishness Doesn't (Want to) See the Bigger Picture

Lack within the Body of Christ often comes from the "lack" of groups willing to submit to what someone else has already in progress. Fear and distrust hinder organizations from connecting for a greater cause. Most of the time, partnering with another organization in the lead role is not appealing or attractive. God may have shown us the same vision; however, what we see in our mind, or how we think it should be carried out, is different from what God sees. Most of the time, we want to be the boss. It's my vision—God gave it to me. We seek to exalt who we are and what we are called to do. We want to be known as the "bigwig." We seek after and thirst for status. And when we get it, we're satisfied. The enemy knows this and uses it to control us.

Most of what God is speaking to His people is not for them to do alone. Rather, they are to join with what He has going on with someone else. It is like the example I shared regarding the big money awarded to help ex-offenders and their families. While the community as a whole benefits, only a few social organizations will get the money to provide the services—Flying HIGH and some others. Why? Because we had no problem submitting to the exact vision of what God wanted and because it was God's timing for us to move forward.

Desire for Status Is Dangerous

Be aware of your internal motivation to get involved or not to get involved with a project or special interest group. Constantly seek God for direction, especially if you are emotionally charged either for or against being involved. The Bible teaches us to be sober minded, and to be vigilant (see 1 Pet. 5:8). Learn to discipline yourself to seek God first and obey His instructions. You may be the missing link to the success of a project initiated by another—or your success in dealing with significant community issues could be stalled by the efforts of someone to exalt you and your work falsely.

The effects of "false exaltation" can manifest in the following way. Groups in the community rise up to bring attention to pressing problems. Politicians (or others in power) grab the leaders of these groups and give them some "crumbs" from the table of recognition—some status, title, or position. They do this to quiet them down. They purposely feed the egos of the leaders. What's the result? The leaders get status, and the community problems don't get solved. These once-passionate leaders then become what I call "kept men." It happens to ministers all the time. *A "kept man" is a man who is under the control of another for his or her own selfish benefit.* Who's controlling you, and why are you permitting it?

Less Fear, More Opportunities

Selfishness blocks us from opportunities God gives to us because it makes us afraid to move along the path He directs. When we follow God's leading, we walk right into the blessings.

After totally surrendering my will to pursue God's perfect will, I had less fear. I was so fearful of not being able to pay bills that whenever a new venture or potential opportunity came along, I'd find myself automatically resisting it. I was so afraid of failing again that I totally had a closed mind instead of an "eye for opportunity." Fear doesn't guide me like it used to, and now I keep running into blessings. In the past, God couldn't get them to me because I was too afraid to follow His lead.

For example, at the time of this writing, our city ranked ninth amongst the most dangerous cities in the U.S. per capita.[1] However, my organization and others that are reaching out to the youth in gangs are not afraid of that statistic. Instead, we aim to change it.

Media reports paint a grim picture of the increase in perverted and distorted crimes committed against people. Young offenders that we meet are sometimes on the brink of exhibiting animal-like behavior because they were raised on the streets by the ways of the streets. The fear of dealing with these mindsets can be paralyzing. But that's where God directed us to go, so each time we trust God for His ability and protection. We're willing to go and do things that others are not willing to do because they are kept away by fear. With the funding we received for servicing ex-offenders, we are in prisons helping ex-offenders prior to their release to the community. Our job is to help them obtain the life skills to succeed and get acclimated to life on the outside. Upon release, we help them obtain jobs and get housing, education, training, and other services they need to succeed.

I recently started a security company to provide security at events where people become quite intoxicated. In the past, fear would have kept me away, but now God's ability through us calms the reveling crowd. The security company is profitable, I might add—God's perfect will.

I am no longer afraid to go places that I wouldn't go before. I don't look at these situations anymore as, "Oh God, no! Not me!" Instead, I see them as opportunities, "Yes, God! Send me!" They are the harvest!

Special Admonition

Before ending this chapter, let's deal with a blessing blocker that must be confronted: Christians involved in sexual relations with, and/or emotional attachment to, others to whom they are not married. God calls this "fornication" or "adultery," even if the persons involved think it's love. Hear this loud and clear: *the only way that a sexual relationship (sexual activity in any form) with another person is love is if the two people involved are committed to God and to one another through marriage.* If not, it is selfishness being expressed through lust with a lot of emotions mixed in! If that's you, realize you don't truly love the person with whom you're sexually active. There is no love without commitment. You are pleasing yourself by having sex with him or her. If you love him or her, then obey God's commands and wait until you are married. Most likely, though, you really don't want to marry this person. And whether you are aware of it or not, you are using him or her solely for your own pleasure. In the name of Jesus Christ, stop it right now!

Conquer Selfishness

Selfishness blocks God from blessing you, and therefore, it blocks you from blessing others. Do you see the seriousness of this? Selfishness is the nature of the devil, and it was your former nature. You now have a new nature that loves God and others, and selfishness no longer has power over you in Christ Jesus! God has given you the power to rule over selfishness, so you do not have to think selfishly another day in your life. *To walk in permanent obedience to God and experience His blessing, you must continually overcome selfish thoughts by resisting fear.*

Action Point

Ask the Holy Spirit to reveal and to help you overcome selfish thinking patterns and behaviors in your life of which you are and are not aware.

Now shout, "In the mighty name of Jesus Christ, I will not be selfish another day in my life! I will enjoy life and have a life in abundance, to the full, until it overflows!"

Endnote

1. See http://www.statestats.com/cit07pop.htm#CITIES.

Selfishness: The Great Manifestation Blocker Study Guide

Study to shew thyself approved unto God, a workman that needeth not to be ashamed, rightly dividing the word of truth.

—2 Timothy 2:15

1. **Selfishness: The Great Manifestation Blocker**

    A. Selfishness is the devil's nature.

    a. James 3:14-16, *"But if you have bitter envy and self-seeking in your hearts...This wisdom does not descend from above, but is earthly, sensual, and demonic..."* (NKJV).

    B. Selfishness exalts its will above God's will.

a. Isaiah 14:13-15, *"...For thou hast said in thine heart...I will exalt my throne above the stars of God...Yet thou shalt be brought down to hell..."*

2. **Selfishness Is a Way of Thinking: Self-Preservation, Self-Gratification, Self-Exaltation**

A. Romans 8:5-8, *"For they that are after the flesh do mind the things of the flesh...they that are in the flesh cannot please God."*

B. 1 John 2:16, *"...the lust of the flesh, and the lust of the eyes, and the pride of life, is not of the Father..."*

C. Selfishness defined: *having too much concern for one's own welfare and interests and little or no concern for God and others.*

D. Selfishness is a form of idolatry.

a. Exodus 20:3, *"Thou shalt have no other gods before Me."*

b. Colossians 3:5, *"Therefore put to death your members which are on the earth ...idolatry"* (NKJV).

3. **Selfishness Examination: Recognize Selfish Thoughts and Motives**

A. Psalm 139:23, *"Search me, O God...know my thoughts."*

B. John 8:32, *"And ye shall know the truth..."*

C. Hebrews 4:12, *"For the word of God is quick...and is a discerner of the thoughts and intents of the heart."*

4. **Get Tough: Discipline Your Thoughts**

A. Proverbs 16:3, *"Commit thy works unto the Lord, and thy thoughts shall be established."*

B. Isaiah 55:7, *"Let the wicked forsake his way, and the unrighteous man his thoughts..."*

C. 2 Corinthians 10:5, *"Casting down imaginations..."*

D. Amos 3:3, *"Can two walk together, except they be agreed?"*

E. Train to pursue love through meditation.

a. 1 Corinthians 13, *"...Love endures long and is patient and kind..."* (AMP).

b. Luke 6:27, *"...Love your enemies, do good to them which hate you..."*

F. The love of God and the Word of God overcome fear and selfishness.

a. 1 John 4:18, *"...but perfect love casteth out fear..."*

b. Ephesians 5:26, *"That He might sanctify and cleanse it with the washing of water by the word."*

c. Acts 19:20, *"So mightily grew the word of God and prevailed."*

5. **Fear + Selfishness = Struggle**

   A. Fear provokes and torments one to be return to old way of thinking.

      a. Genesis 18:15, *"Then Sarah denied, saying, I laughed not; for she was afraid..."*

      b. 1 John 4:18, *"...because fear hath torment..."*

   B. Fear pressures us to take things into our own hands.

   C. 1 Samuel 18:29, *"And Saul was yet the more afraid of David; and Saul became David's enemy continually."*

   D. Fear is used by satan to keep the focus on self-preservation, gratification, and exaltation.

      a. Matthew 4:1-11, *"...And when the tempter came to Him* [Jesus], *he said, If Thou be the Son of God, command that these stones be made bread..."*

      b. James 1:14, *"But every man is tempted, when he is drawn away of his own lust, and enticed."*

6. **Overcoming the Struggle**

   A. The struggle is a result of not fully committing to God's leading.

      a. Deuteronomy 28:15-68, *"...if thou wilt not hearken unto the voice of the Lord thy God, to observe to do all His commandments and His statutes...that all these curses shall come upon thee, and overtake thee...*"

B. The world we live in requires Christians to live a life of constant discipline.

a. 1 Corinthians 15:57-58, "*...be ye stedfast, unmoveable, always abounding in the work of the Lord...*"

b. 1 John 4:4, "*...and have overcome them: because greater is He that is in you, than he that is in the world.*"

c. Philippians 4:13, "*I can do all things through Christ which strengtheneth me.*"

C. Follow after God regardless of circumstances and situations, emotions and popular opinion.

a. 1 John 5:5, "*Who is he that overcometh the world, but he that believeth that Jesus is the Son of God?*"

b. 2 Corinthians 4:18, "*While we look not at the things which are seen...*"

D. Jesus is our example.

a. Matthew 4:1-11, "*...the devil...saith unto Him, All these things will I give Thee, if Thou wilt fall down and worship me. Then saith Jesus unto him, Get thee hence, Satan: for it is written, Thou shalt worship the Lord thy God, and Him only shalt thou serve...*"

b. Matthew 26:39, *"...My Father, if it is possible, let this cup pass away from Me; nevertheless, not what I will [not what I desire], but as You will and desire"* (AMP).

7. **Selfishness Produces Lack**

A. Psalm 34:10, *"The young lions do lack, and suffer hunger: but they that seek the Lord shall not want any good thing."*

B. Proverbs 6:32, *"But whoso committeth adultery with a woman lacketh understanding: he that doeth it destroyeth his own soul."*

C. Proverbs 28:27, *"He that giveth unto the poor shall not lack: but he that hideth his eyes shall have many a curse."*

8. **Selfishness Doesn't (Want to) See the Bigger Picture**

A. Assignments in the Body of Christ are most often connected to one another.

a. Genesis 11:6, *"Behold, the people is one, and they have all one language...and now nothing will be restrained from them, which they have imagined to do."*

b. Romans 8:28, *"...all things work together...to them who are the called according to His purpose."*

c. Ephesians 4:16, *"From whom the whole body fitly joined together and compacted by that which every joint supplieth..."*

d. Luke 16:12, *"And if ye have not been faithful in that which is another man's, who shall give you that which is your own?"*

B. Beware of internal motivation. Seek God for direction.

a. Genesis 25:19-34, 27:1-44: Jacob and Esau

b. 1 Peter 5:8, *"Be sober, be vigilant..."*

c. Romans 12:3, *"...not to think of himself more highly than he ought to think..."*

9. Less Fear, More Opportunities

A. Selfishness makes us afraid to follow after God's Kingdom opportunities.

a. Judges 7:3, *"...Whosoever is fearful and afraid, let him return and depart early from mount Gilead..."*

b. Jonah 1:3, *"But Jonah rose up to flee unto Tarshish from the presence of the Lord..."*

c. Matthew 9:37, *"...The harvest truly is plenteous, but the labourers are few."*

B. Blessings and provision are along the path of God's perfect will.

a. Genesis 22:8, 13-14, *"...a ram caught in a thicket by his horns...Abraham called the name of that place Jehovah-jireh..."*

b. Genesis 42:25, *"...restore every man's money into his sack, and to give them provision for the way..."*

c. Luke 22:35, *"...When I sent you without purse, and scrip, and shoes, lacked ye any thing? And they said, Nothing."*

C. Yes, God! Send Me!

a. Isaiah 6:8, *"I heard the voice of the Lord, saying, Whom shall I send...Then said I, Here am I; send me."*

b. John 20:21, *"Then said Jesus to them again, Peace be unto you: as My Father hath sent Me, even so send I you."*

10. Conquer Selfishness

A. You have a new nature.

a. Ezekiel 36:26, *"A new heart also will I give you...and I will take away the stony heart..."*

b. 1 Corinthians 2:16, *"But we have the mind of Christ."*

c. 2 Corinthians 5:17, *"...if any man be in Christ, he is a new creature..."*

d. Prayer: Ask the Holy Spirit to reveal and help you overcome selfish thinking and behaviors of which you are and are not aware.

11. Declarations

A. I will think of others, and I will pursue their interests and do things for their advantage!

B. In the mighty name of Jesus Christ, I will not be selfish another day in my life! I will enjoy life and have life in abundance, to the full, until it overflows!

Notes

Notes

Chapter 7

Guard Your Heart

YOUR HEART IS THE ESSENCE of you. It's the real you. It is the place where life flows from you, both physically and spiritually. Your physical heart pumps blood throughout your entire body, giving life to it (see Lev. 17:14). When the blood stops flowing, your body stops living. Your spiritual heart, your spirit or inner man, produces the springs of life (see Prov. 4:23). It creates spiritual things like thoughts, emotions, and words. It also houses and causes to grow whatever is placed in it. *Basically, God made your heart to be your command center to produce and direct your life while on this earth and into eternity.*

So we see why God focuses and places such value on your heart: the condition of your heart impacts the condition of your life, both now and in the future. God also knows that the condition of your heart is the one thing that will determine if you will continue to walk with Him in permanent obedience to His perfect will. Therefore, He gives us these important instructions: "*Watch* [watchful, ever awake and on the alert] *over your heart with all diligence, for from it flow the springs of life"* (Prov. 4:23 NASB). The same verse in the Amplified Bible tells us to, *"Keep and guard your heart with all vigilance and* ***above all that you guard,*** *for out of it flow the springs of life."* God says, *"above all that you guard,"* you should guard your heart. Did you get it? Above all! Above everything! *You must guard your heart because it determines whether you will continue to walk in God's perfect will for your life!* There is nothing more important than the condition of your heart while on this earth. Guarding your heart will keep you walking in permanent obedience to God and keep you in His perfect will!

How do you watch over and guard your heart so you can walk every day in permanent obedience to God? *Guard your heart by keeping it in constant motion to please God and to pursue a closer relationship with Him.*

Our "spiritual" hearts were meant to be in constant motion. Like our physical hearts are in constant motion, *we must constantly pursue our love relationship with God.* We were made to love God with all of our heart, all of our soul, all of our mind, and all of our strength. Not at any time can we stop our pursuit of God and His Kingdom advancement, no more than our physical heart can stop beating. This is what Jesus meant when He said, *"Seek first God's kingdom and what God wants. Then all your other needs will be met as well"* (Matt. 6:33 NCV), and *"Blessed are those who hunger and thirst for righteousness, for they shall be satisfied"* (Matt. 5:6 NASB). When a man is hungry or thirsty, he does not stop pursuing food and drink until he is satisfied. That's the kind of pursuit God is talking about, where there is a hunger and thirst for Him—to know Him more through His Word; to be a channel of His love to bless others; to walk in the fullness of all His Son's blood has accomplished; to be more like Him and walk even as Jesus walked (see 1 John 2:6)! You must come to the place where this is your heart's sincere desire, or as God calls it in Romans 12:1, "*...your reasonable service*" of worship.

Pursuing God keeps our hearts pure (see 1 John 3:3) because nothing else has the opportunity to enter into it. *When your heart is in constant motion pursuing a deeper love for God, it is simultaneously flushing out all fear and selfishness* (see 1 John 4:18). It's like being totally in love, where even the very thought of doing something disloyal to the relationship is repulsive. This is true devotion. Think of true devotion in the way we behave toward babies. When we have a baby, everything in our lives focuses on taking care of her (or him). It's natural for us to do so. The baby and her needs take priority over anything else. We think of her in the midst of everything going on in our lives. The baby becomes a part of our lives because we love her and are constantly seeking to meet her needs. One could say we are truly devoted to her.

However, when we focus our hearts only on ourselves, either on purpose or by being distracted by other things, we stop making progress in our love relationship with God, and we return to selfish living. This is the place of disobedience. *Disobedience can always be traced back to some selfish motive.*

Leaving Behind Childish Things

Sometimes people think they have a right to keep a little part of their lives for themselves to do what they want. They justify this right by convincing themselves that they deserve it because they work hard and are always doing so much for others. On other occasions they self-righteously compare themselves with others and mistakenly believe that they are better than most, so they have a right to have some selfish pleasures. (Those who struggle with any sort of addiction tend to have this mentality.) They justify what they know is destructive behavior and continue to violate their conscience by continuing to do what they know is wrong. All the while, the enemy is laughing because he is successfully using selfish desires to destroy them. If this resembles you in any way, then I believe God would have me say these words to you: *grow up and leave behind this kind of childish, selfish thinking!*

Press forward toward maturity, give all of yourself to God daily, and hold no area back. *He will give to you whatever you give to Him.* If you fully give Him your life, God promises to give you a full, abundant life in return as the Lord Jesus Christ says it in John 10:10: *"...I came that they may have and enjoy life, and have it in abundance (to the full, till it overflows)"* (AMP). Why wouldn't we want to enjoy our life and have it *"in abundance, to the full, till it overflows"*? *If you are not enjoying your life, it's a sign that you have not fully surrendered to His perfect will for you.*

You were made to live every breath of every day madly in love with God. This means that your heart was designed to always pursue His desires for your life. This is how you were originally created. *You were made to live completely surrendered and completely obedient to God without any fear.* When at any time you turn your heart toward yourself in selfishness or fear and willfully seek your own interests, you stop the power of God from operating through you, and you are left to operate in your own ability. I believe this is the greatest struggle for the Body of Christ right now. Many are constantly wavering between pleasing God and pleasing themselves. Wavering is a result of what Jesus succinctly said, we have "left our first love" (see Rev. 2:4). When we allow our love for God to grow cold, our love for ourselves grows stronger. And this is not the good life.

Action Point

Simply ask the Lord Jesus Christ to help you give your life totally to Him daily so that He can give you the good life He totally wants for you.

Guard Your Heart Study Guide

Study to shew thyself approved unto God, a workman that needeth not to be ashamed, rightly dividing the word of truth.

—2 Timothy 2:15

Guard Your Heart

1. **Your Heart Is the Essence of Who You Are.**
2. **Two Hearts: Spiritual and Physical**

   A. The physical heart pumps blood to give life.

      a. Leviticus 17:14, *"For it is the life of all flesh; the blood of it is for the life thereof..."*

   B. The spiritual heart produces springs of life.

a. Proverbs 4:23, *"...for out of it flow the springs of life"* (AMP).

3. **Your Heart Is the Command Center to Produce and Direct Your Life.**

   A. Proverbs 4:23, *"Keep and guard your heart with all vigilance...for out of it flow the springs of life"* (AMP).

   B. Proverbs 14:30, *"...A sound heart is the life of the flesh..."*

   C. Matthew 12:34, *"...for out of the abundance of the heart the mouth speaketh."*

4. **Love and Pursue God With All Your Heart.**

   A. Matthew 5:6, *"...Blessed are they which do hunger and thirst after righteousness..."*

   B. Matthew 6:33, *"...But seek ye first the kingdom of God, and His righteousness..."*

   C. Desire to be more like Jesus.

      a. 1 John 2:6, *"...walk, even as He* [Jesus] *walked."*

      b. Romans 8:29, *"...to be conformed to the image of His Son..."*

      c. Romans 12:2, *"...be ye transformed by the renewing of your mind..."*

5. **Pursuing God Keeps Our Hearts Pure and Develops True Devotion Toward Him.**

    A. 2 Timothy 2:22, *"...but follow righteousness...with them that call on the Lord out of a pure heart."*

    B. 1 John 3:3, *"And every man that hath this hope in him purifieth himself, even as He is pure."*

    C. 1 John 4:18, *"...He that feareth is not made perfect in love..."*

6. **Abandon Childish, Selfish Thinking.**

    A. The self-righteous justify their rights to enjoy some selfish pleasures.

        a. Romans 10:3, *"...and going about to establish their own righteousness, have not submitted themselves unto the righteousness of God."*

    B. Press forward toward maturity in totally submitting your whole self to God daily.

        a. Romans 12:1, *"...present your bodies a living sacrifice, holy, acceptable unto God..."*

        b. Philippians 3:14, *"I press toward the mark for the prize of the high calling of God in Christ Jesus."*

        c. 2 Peter 3:18, *"But grow in grace, and in the knowledge of our Lord and Saviour Jesus Christ..."*

C. A fully submitted life enjoys an abundant life in return.

a. Deuteronomy 28:1-14, *"...all these blessings shall come on thee, and overtake thee, if thou shalt hearken unto the voice of the Lord thy God..."*

b. John 10:10, *"...I came that they may have and enjoy life, and have it in abundance (to the full, till it overflows)"* (AMP).

7. **Stop, Stopping the Power.**

A. Selfishness and fear stop the power of God from operating through you and leave you to operate in your own ability.

a. Galatians 5:26, *"Let us not become vainglorious and self-conceited, competitive and challenging and provoking and irritating to one another, envying and being jealous of one another"* (AMP).

B. Wavering is a result of leaving one's first love.

a. James 1:6, *"...For he that wavereth is like a wave of the sea driven with the wind and tossed."*

b. Revelation 2:4, *"...because thou hast left thy first love."*

Notes

Notes

CHAPTER 8

Living the Good Life—for Real

THE DEPTH OF RELATIONSHIP with your Heavenly Father is determined by your choices. This is why God said in James 4:8, *"Draw near to God and He will draw near to you..."* (NASB). God respects the dominion or control He gave you on the earth; therefore, He allows you to choose the depth of relationship you want with Him. If a man desires to live on earth without a relationship with God, He respects the authority He gave man on earth by allowing him to do it. This man is called a *"fool"* (Ps. 14:1), but nonetheless, God loves the man enough that He will not violate His Word nor the man's choice. Here's a difficult truth: people can live on this earth without God, then die and go to hell because of God's love—His commitment and devotion to respect their decisions—for them. Man determines his own destiny while on this earth, not God. God desires that all men be saved from eternal separation from

Him (see 1 Tim. 2:4); this is why He sent Jesus (see John 3:16). At any time a man decides to turn his heart toward God and love Him with all his heart, God is right there ready to receive him. But He will not force a relationship with anyone.

Are you getting the point? You determine your closeness with your Heavenly Father on a day-to-day basis. He gave you the right to be as close to Him as you want to be, or as far from Him as you want. However, He never changes (see Heb. 13:8). He is always pursuing His love for you; He is always ready to talk with you; He is always willing to help you; and He will always be loyal to you. This is why He requires loyalty from you. *He requires it because He doesn't* ***force*** *you to be loyal.* Loyalty toward God has got to be something you want to do. It has got to come from the very core of you—your heart. It should not be something that you feel you "have to do," but, rather, something you "get to do."

You Gotta Want It!

Athletes talk about "playing with heart!" or "you gotta want it!" What they are saying is their desire to win has more influence on their performance than their physical abilities. They know there is an intangible quality that enables them to overcome any obstacle and how much "heart," (i.e., desire) they play with determines how much success they experience. This is what Jesus was talking about when He said, *"For this reason I say to you, her sins, which are many, have been forgiven, for she loved much; but he who is forgiven little, loves little"* (Luke 7:47 NASB).

Those of us who really have an understanding of what we were before Christ, and where we would be if not for Him, know what He is talking about. It's almost like we're in a constant state of shock over the fact that the Lord Jesus Christ Himself would even want to have anything to do with us. We just can't help but to have much love for Him. We are also totally in awe that we get to have a relationship with Him as well as the opportunity to prove our loyalty. This is simply beyond our wildest dreams. As a result, our loyalty to Him is something *we should eagerly desire to pursue* with all our heart, soul, mind, and strength, no matter what we face or go through. I believe this is how the early apostles felt in Acts 5:40-42, *when after being beaten, "they went on their way from the presence of the Council,* ***rejoicing that they had been considered worthy to suffer shame for His name****"* (NASB). Oh, thank God for His great mercy that He has lavished upon us!

Remaining loyal to God and keeping your heart pure before Him is as natural for you, His child, as collecting honey is to bees. No one has to force you. These come naturally because it is now your new nature to do them. *You are a loyal, pure-hearted person.* That's the real you in Christ Jesus. Always be mindful that God has made you a new creature in Christ Jesus, and you now possess His good nature (see 2 Cor. 5:17). Remind yourself occasionally, *"I have my Heavenly Father's good nature; therefore, I am a loyal, pure-hearted person!"*

Not only does God give us His good nature, but He also gives us a helper, the Holy Spirit, the Spirit of Truth. It's the

Spirit of Jesus Christ Himself (see John 14:6). Jesus said, *"I will ask the Father, and He will give you another Helper that He may be with you forever; that is the Spirit of truth, whom the world cannot receive, because it does not see Him or know Him, but you know Him, because He abides with you and* ***will be in you****"* (John 14:16-17 NASB).

So because we possess His good nature and He has given us His Holy Spirit as our helper, our part becomes easy. In order to remain loyal to Him and keep our hearts pure, we simply must 1.) eagerly desire to do so, and 2.) learn to be led by the Holy Spirit.

Be Led by the Holy Spirit

Jesus said in John 10,

> *"...And the sheep listen to the voice of the shepherd. He calls His own sheep by name and leads them out. When He brings all His sheep out, He goes ahead of them, and they follow Him because* ***they know His voice****. But they will never follow a stranger. They will run away from Him because they don't know His voice"* (John 10:3-5 NCV).
>
> *"I am the good shepherd. I know My sheep, and My sheep know Me, just as the Father knows Me, and I know the Father. I give My life for the sheep"* (John 10:14 NCV).
>
> *"My sheep listen to My voice; I know them, and they follow Me"* (John 10:27 NCV).

Now listen to Jesus carefully. He said, "*...they know His voice.*" I didn't say this; Jesus did. *"They know"* means you, and *"His voice,"* means the voice of Jesus, which we discovered is the voice of God, because Jesus only speaks to us from what He has learned from the Father (see John 8:38). Plainly, Jesus is saying, "You know My voice." Every believer born of God knows the voice of God. It comes naturally for us to know it because we have the same Holy Spirit as He does. Likewise, you didn't have to try to learn the voice of your mother through some complicated process. It was natural for you to recognize it.

Perhaps you're thinking, "I don't know if I hear God or not." You do! Jesus said you do! Perhaps you have not developed your faith to the point where you have the confidence to know it's Him when He is speaking to you. Thankfully, this issue is easily resolved by developing your confidence in God's Word. Get yourself into agreement with Him by saying His Word. *"Jesus is my Shepherd, I know His voice, and the voice of a stranger, I will not follow"* (see John 10:3-5). After that, simply believe in what you are saying, and from this point on, expect to hear God loud and clear. In a short time, you will be hearing His voice with confidence. It happened this way with me, and it only comes through practice.

The Holy Spirit will speak to you about everything in your life. From the smallest to the greatest things, He wants to be involved and offer His assistance. Remember, He is an expert on your heart and knows exactly what will fulfill you and what will harm you. *He knows you better than you know you.*

Therefore, He desires to teach, lead, guide, and counsel you in all areas of your life. Isaiah 48:17 says He is *"...the Lord your God, who teaches you to profit, who leads you in the way you should go"* (NASB). He will also reveal to you things to come. We sometimes call these premonitions, but really they are the Holy Spirit giving us insight into the future.

Hear and Do

Can a good teacher teach someone who is not willing to learn? Surprisingly, the answer is yes. However, the teacher is limited to instructing the student through experiences. This means he or she must allow the unwilling student to go through hard times, and then use his or her bad experiences as opportunities to teach good lessons. And take it from me, learning by experience can be merciless. My "learning center" experience is a perfect example. What's the better way to learn? *Hear and do!*

The ability to hear from God and do what He says is what makes us different from those of the world. Our relationship with Jesus Christ connects us with the living God, so we can hear and obey Him. *If you can't hear from God—you're no different than the world.* The world is most afraid of our ability to hear from God, and our enemy, satan, has attacked it the most. "You heard from whom? God? OK, you must be crazy," they reason. That perception has influenced the Body of Christ to become a little shy on speaking up and saying, "I hear and obey God."

In my *pollutedness*, I did not hear God like I used to hear Him. A turning point for me was when I started believing again. I believe I now hear Him loud and clear all the time.

Our ability to hear and do exactly as God has instructed is such a priority with Him. Think about it. Imagine you run an organization focused on doing good in the earth, and there are tons of issues coming, projects to be done, and needs to be met. When you have critical instructions to be carried out, you're going to seek out the staff members who you know are absolutely going to get the job done correctly and in a timely manner.

Even our military is trained to hear the commands and follow through without hesitation, distraction, or discussion. They are trained to get it done and get it done now.

Examine your response pattern to God's instructions. Are you a little lazy—too slow to move? Do you tend to be overzealous—moving too fast or taking shortcuts? Are you afraid—procrastinating for fear of losing something, caught up in self-preservation? You want to respond to God in the same manner in which you desire Him to respond to you: on time with exactly what you need to be done.

Let's give careful attention again to what Jesus has to say: *"My sheep listen to My voice; I know them, and they follow Me."* Did you catch it? *"My sheep listen to My voice."* Jesus is saying, "My sheep listen, or in other words, they do what I tell them."

Then He says, *"I know them, and they follow Me."* He knows the sheep that will do what He says.

Remember the parable of the talents in Matthew 25:14-30. Look how the master gave to them in verse 15: *"And to one he gave five talents, to another two, and to another one, to* ***each according to his own ability****; and immediately he went on a journey"* (NKJV). How did he give to them? "Each according to his own ability." We have to ask: ability to do what?" *Their ability to do exactly what he said to do with it.* It is vital to understand that your ability to do exactly what God tells you to do with what he gives you will determine how much He will put under your influence.

Two of them did what the master told them, and he increased their possessions. *"The lord said to him, 'Well done,* ***good and faithful*** *servant; you were faithful over a few things, I will make you ruler over many things. Enter into the joy of your lord'"* (Matt. 25:21 NKJV). The other one willfully disobeyed because he was afraid, and he hid his talent. *"But his lord answered and said to him, 'You* ***wicked and lazy*** *servant, you knew that I reap where I have not sown, and gather where I have not scattered seed'"* (Matt. 25:26 NKJV). Now, which do you want the Master, the Lord Jesus Christ, to call you one day? "Good and faithful" or "wicked and lazy"?

Know this: if you do not develop an ear to hear Him and a mind to work, you're not going to fulfill God's perfect will for your life. Why? Whatever God tells you to do is going to take some amount of physical effort and work to accomplish. There is no room for laziness in the Kingdom of God. Work is a constant activity in the Kingdom. It is not the busyness we know or the day-to-day grind we go through to make money but work and effort that is a direct result of what we have heard our Heavenly Father instruct us to do. That's what Flying HIGH, Inc. is to me—it's not a job, but the work God has given me to do in the earth.

Hear and do! In a nutshell, this describes how you show love and devotion in your relationship with your Heavenly Father. Listen to Jesus in John 14:23-24; *"...If anyone loves Me, he will keep My Word; and My Father will love him, and We will come to him and make Our abode with him. He who does not love Me does not keep My words; and the word which you hear is not Mine, but the Father who sent Me"* (NASB). It is the foundation of your life in Christ to hear God's voice through His written Word and be led by the Holy Spirit to quickly do what He says. This is how you live as Jesus lived in this earth. *This is our part in our love relationship with our Heavenly Father. It is how we express our love to Him.* It's so simple: Listen to His voice; then do what He tells you!

This is why Jesus said, *"If you love Me, you will keep My commandments"* (John 14:15 NASB). Now let's take the religious thinking out of this statement. It is basic common sense. If you really love somebody and he or she asks you to do something, it's natural not only to consent to do it but also to be eager. If a child really loves his parents, he demonstrates his love by his willing obedience. Obedience is an expression of love. Let me say that again in case you missed it: *obedience is an expression of love*. If you love your Heavenly Father, obedience comes naturally to you. Love and obedience are like two peas in a pod. That's all God is looking for—someone who will hear His voice and do whatever it takes to obey. It's what Adam failed to do but what Jesus did perfectly.

In the Old Testament, God uses the word *hearken* over and over when speaking to His people. To me, *hearken* means to be ever-ready to hear God's voice at any time, about anything. God wants a people who will *hearken.* However, when we have areas in our life that we keep from Him, we are not ever-ready to hear Him. We don't want to hear what God says to us because we are unwilling to change.

Why should God speak to someone He knows won't listen? If He does speak to that person, his or her heart would harden like Pharaoh's (see Exod. 7:14; 8:32; 9:7). This is what happens when we hear God, either His voice or written command, and in childish stubbornness refuse to do it. It has a hardening effect on our hearts like the sun on clay. Thankfully, in His great mercy, our Heavenly Father never leaves us and waits to speak when we finally decide we want to change.

Jesus instructs us to develop this eager desire to hear God at any time about anything. It is a desire that says, "I've got to hear God's voice today," and "I have to find out what God wants done in this situation." *Whether it's the voice of the Holy*

Spirit inside you or God speaking to you in His written Word, you must want to hear and want to obey to become an excellent hearer.

Jesus also instructs us to develop an eager desire to do what He says quickly. Therefore, *you must deliberately put effort into acting on what He tells you, immediately, in order to become an excellent doer.* Through repetition and practice, military soldiers have trained themselves to be willing and ready to hastily obey a superior's command. Likewise, you must allow God to develop you to the point where you can hear Him clearly and then do what He tells you quickly, even when you're under pressure or out in the hustle-bustle of this world. This is the place of maturity and practical, day-to-day reality that you want to get to, but it will take diligent practice on your part. You'll be amazed how quickly things in your life start to improve. The Holy Spirit will help you in any and every situation.

Commit and declare to your Heavenly Father frequently, *"I hear and do because I love You!"*

Listen, Then Talk

One way to practice hearing God's voice is to purposely set time aside in the day to meditate on His Word and listen to what He has to say to you. What does God have to say about your situation, decision, or circumstance? Rather than spend your time doing all the talking, simply invite God's presence through praise and then quiet down and let Him speak. He knows all about your needs and problems without you saying a word (see Matt. 6:8). Furthermore, what He says to you is much more important than what you say to Him, because what He says to you is the final authority in your situation. For example, if He tells you, "All is well," then all is well in your situation, regardless of what it looks like. If He leads you to specific Scriptures, then that is His Word to you regarding your situation.

Your part then becomes to quickly get your words into agreement with His Word. *Therefore, the time for you to speak about your situation is only after you hear what He says regarding it.* Proceed to praise Him for all being well, and then quickly start declaring, "All is well." Declare the Scriptures He shows you. He wants you to declare *whatever He tells you about your situation, and He wants you to do it quickly.* Do you see His pattern for you? He speaks to you, then you speak and declare the same words about your situation, quickly, regardless of what it looks like or how long it takes to change. This will cause your situation to submit to your God-restored power and conform to the image of His spoken Word. This is why satan is constantly trying to distract you from spending time with God, attempting to get you to doubt God's Word. He does so because he knows one word from God can truly change your life!

I highly recommend Gloria Copeland's book, *God's Will Is Prosperity*. It will greatly help you stand on the Word of God until you have received all God has promised you in every area of your life.

Write Down What God Says to You

This is so simple, but so very important: keep a notebook solely for writing down what He says and the Scriptures He shows you. Make sure to keep things dated. *You must write down what He says to ensure you don't forget it and to ensure you can accurately do it.* This is how you practice hearing and doing. It will be there for you to look at and meditate on. God will tell you things that He wants you to practice daily and incorporate into your lifestyle. He speaks simply, but we must think through what He says to squeeze out all the understanding we can from it. Take the time to do this very important thing! Write it down so you can meditate and then accurately execute!

Declare Thou Unto Me!

One of the first things God did for me to help me turn things around was to remind me to exercise my authority. I was dealing with a lot of issues: creditors, debt, possible bankruptcy and foreclosure. It was overwhelming. I had become like Job, whining and crying about how bad things were, instead of using my God-given authority and dominating over my emotions and the situation.

Because we are born again into the family of God, we can exercise the authority given to us through Jesus Christ. Through Him, we are the "acting authority" on this earth, which means we can rule over earthly things—over ourselves and our environment (our world). It's not some magical phenomena; it's what the Lord Jesus Christ accomplished for us. Here's how He put it in Matthew 28:18: *"All authority has been given to Me in heaven and on earth"* (NASB). The Lord Jesus Christ, the last Adam, came and restored to us what the first Adam lost—our God-given power to rule over ourselves and our environment.

Look at what God said to Job while he was in his desperate situation, *"Gird up thy loins now like a man: I will demand of thee, and **declare thou unto Me**"* (Job 40:7). Did you catch that last part? *"...Declare thou unto Me."* Basically God said, "Be strong and act like a man: Stop whining, shut your friends up, and start declaring My Word over your situation and yourself."

I was so driven and needy that I talked too much around people and around God. I was always saying something around people, trying to hit the right nerve so they could help me out or hook me up. And my prayers were more like a one-ring communication circus with me as the ringmaster *and* the clown. My so-called "fervent prayer" meant I got louder and more aggressive until I reached an emotional tizzy. The more emotional I got, the more "effective" I thought I was in prayer. God said to me, "Shut up. Be quiet. Only speak the Word I give you."

I was saying many words, but they were powerless and had no authority. My prayers had a form of godliness (see 2 Tim. 3:5), but no power. They were backed by thoughts of fear instead of faith. My words said, "I hope He hears me and does something this time." I had no firm revelation that Jesus had already accomplished it for me. I was so busy trying to make things happen that I couldn't hear God saying, "It's already done because of my Son. Believe in what He has done for you and declare My Word as done in your life." For example, in the middle of my desperate situation, God spoke to me to believe and regularly declare Second Corinthians 9:8 (AMP). Here's how He showed me to say it: "Because of all Jesus has done, I declare that God has made all grace, every favor, and earthly blessing come to me in abundance, so that always and under all circumstances and whatever the need, I am self-sufficient and possess enough to require no aid or support, and I am furnished in abundance for every good work and charitable donation."

Most of my prayer time is now spent meditating and listening and then saying and doing what I hear. I snapped out of the "quick-fix" mentality—the lottery mentality—that says, "Just maybe, maybe one day, I'm going to hit it big." Instead, I disciplined myself to change from that way of thinking and get into the Kingdom of God's way of thinking. It's a consistent, never-ending process. Listen. Meditate. Declare. Listen. Meditate. Declare. What does God say about it? What are His instructions? Declare and establish His Word—speak it out loud!

The Good Life takes time but before you know it, you and God will be living it together. All it requires is a disciplined life of meditating in His Word, listening to Him and then doing what He tells you. *For I am confident of this very thing, that He who began a good work in you will perfect it, until the day of Christ Jesus* (Phil. 1:6 NASB).

Closing Prayer

Heavenly Father, I declare that the Scriptures and insight shared within the pages of this book will act as a guiding light along the good life that You have designed for me to live. I love You, Lord, with all my heart, soul, mind, and strength, and I declare Thy Kingdom come, Thy perfect will be done in and through my life—in Jesus's name, Amen!

Living the Good Life—for Real Study Outline

Study to shew thyself approved unto God, a workman that needeth not to be ashamed, rightly dividing the word of truth.

—2 Timothy 2:15

1. Determine Your Closeness With Your Heavenly Father

A. James 4:8, *"Draw nigh to God, and He will draw nigh to you…"*

B. God is always pursuing His love for us.

a. Isaiah 55:7, *"…and let him return unto the Lord, and He will have mercy upon him; and to our God, for He will abundantly pardon."*

b. Jeremiah 3:1, "*...but thou hast played the harlot with many lovers; yet return again to me, saith the Lord.*"

c. John 3:16, "*For God so loved the world, that He gave His only begotten Son...*"

i. Hebrews 13:8, "*Jesus Christ the same yesterday, and to day, and for ever.*"

2. You Gotta Want It: Eagerly Desire to Be Loyal to God

A. Luke 7:47, "*...Her sins, which are many, are forgiven; for she loved much: but to whom little is forgiven, the same loveth little.*"

B. Remain loyal to God in the face of adversity.

a. Acts 5:40-42, "*...they commanded that they should not speak in the name of Jesus, and let them go...And daily in the temple, and in every house, they ceased not to teach and preach Jesus Christ.*"

b. 2 Timothy 3:12, "*Yea, and all that will live godly in Christ Jesus shall suffer persecution.*"

C. The Holy Spirit helps us.

a. John 14:16-17, "*And I will pray the Father, and He shall give you another Comforter, that He may abide with you for ever...*"

3. Be Led by the Holy Spirit: Know His Voice

A. John 10:3-5, *"...the sheep follow him: for they know his voice..."*

B. John 10:14, *"I am the good shepherd, and know My sheep, and am known of Mine."*

C. John 10:27, *"My sheep hear My voice, and I know them, and they follow Me."*

D. Romans 8:14, *"For as many as are led by the Spirit of God, they are the sons of God."*

E. The Holy Spirit will speak to you about everything in your life.

   a. Romans 8:27, *"And He that searcheth the hearts knoweth what is the mind of the Spirit..."*

   b. Isaiah 48:17, *"...I am the Lord thy God which teacheth thee to profit, which leadeth thee by the way that thou shouldest go."*

   c. John 16:13, *"Howbeit when He, the Spirit of truth, is come, He will guide you into all truth..."*

4. **Hear and Do**

A. Hearing from God makes the difference.

B. Relationship with Jesus Christ connects us with the living God.

a. John 14:6, *"Jesus saith unto him, I am the way, the truth, and the life: no man cometh unto the Father, but by Me."*

C. Our ability to hear and do is a priority with God.

a. James 1:19, *"Wherefore, my beloved brethren, let every man be swift to hear, slow to speak, slow to wrath."*

D. Examine your response pattern to God's instructions.

a. Jonah 1:1-3, *"Now the word of the Lord came unto Jonah...But Jonah rose up to flee unto Tarshish from the presence of the Lord..."*

b. Jeremiah 1:6, *"Then said I, Ah, Lord God! behold, I cannot speak: for I am a child."*

c. Luke 1:38, *"And Mary said, Behold the handmaid of the Lord; be it unto me according to thy word..."*

E. God knows those who will do what He instructs.

a. Parable of the talents: Matthew 25:14-30.

i. Instructions given according to individual ability.

ii. The faithful rewarded with greater influence.

F. Show love and devotion to God by hearing and doing.

a. John 14:23-24, *"...If a man love Me, he will keep My words..."*

b. John 2:5, *"...Whatsoever He saith unto you, do it."*

c. John 14:15, *"If ye love Me, keep My commandments."*

G. Hearken: be ever-ready to hear God's voice at any time, about anything.

H. The hardened heart does not hearken.

a. Exodus 7:14, 8:32, 9:7, *"...And Pharaoh hardened his heart at this time also, neither would he let the people go..."*

b. Matthew 19:8, *"...Moses because of the hardness of your hearts suffered you to put away your wives: but from the beginning it was not so."*

I. Become an excellent hearer and doer.

a. James 1:22, *"But be ye doers of the word, and not hearers only..."*

5. Listen, Then Talk: Repeat What God Speaks

A. Practice hearing God's voice.

B. Get your words into agreement with God's Word.

a. Matthew 6:8, *"...for your Father knoweth what things ye have need of, before ye ask Him."*

6. **Write Down What God Says to You**

   A. Habakkuk 2:2-3, *"…Write the vision, and make it plain upon tables, that he may run that readeth it…"*

   B. Write it down, meditate, and execute!

7. **"Declare Thou Unto Me": Exercise Your God-given Authority**

   A. Matthew 28:18, *"And Jesus came and spake unto them, saying, All power is given unto Me in heaven and in earth."*

   B. Job 40:7, *"I will demand of thee, and declare thou unto me."*

   C. Avoid fear-based prayers that are full of emotional words, but no power.

      a. 2 Timothy 3:5, *"Having a form of godliness, but denying the power thereof: from such turn away."*

   D. Pray with faith and confidence.

      a. 2 Corinthians 9:8, *"And God is able to make all grace abound toward you, that ye, always having all sufficiency in all things, may abound to every good work…"*

      b. Hebrews 10:35, *"Cast not away therefore your confidence, which hath great recompence of reward."*

c. 1 John 5:14-15, *"And this is the confidence that we have in Him, that, if we ask any thing according to His will, He heareth us..."*

E. Listen. Meditate. Declare.

Notes

Notes

About the Author

JEFFREY M. MAGADA is a *professional potential developer* who has 20 years experience in social and community service. He is the founder and executive director of Flying HIGH, Inc., a pioneering 501(c)(3) tax-exempt community development community service organization dedicated to developing the potential of young people and adults. Since 1988, he has been a pioneer in establishing effective community services both in the private and public sectors. Prior to Flying HIGH, Inc., he was the supervisor of the Austintown police department's juvenile diversion program. In 1995, the Austintown program was selected as a model program in the state of Ohio for its effective work with at-risk young people. Most recently, Mr. Magada has been instrumental in securing over a million dollars in federal and state grant awards for his community. He was born and raised in Youngstown, Ohio, where he currently resides with his family.

Contact Information

Jeffrey M. Magada
P.O. Box 4740
Youngstown, Ohio 44515

E-mail: jeff@flyinghighinc.org

Phone: 330-881-9876

Flying HIGH, Inc.
P.O. Box 4971
Youngstown, Ohio 44515

Phone: 330-797-3995

Fax: 330-270-9492

Web site: www.flyinghighinc.org